# PARENTING THE TEENAGE BRAIN

## Understanding a Work in Progress

### Sheryl Feinstein

Rowman & Littlefield Education
Lanham, Maryland • Toronto • Plymouth, UK
2007

Published in the United States of America
by Rowman & Littlefield Education
A Division of Rowman & Littlefield Publishers, Inc.
A wholly owned subsidiary of The Rowman & Littlefield Publishing
Group, Inc.
4501 Forbes Boulevard, Suite 200, Lanham, Maryland 20706
www.rowmaneducation.com

Estover Road
Plymouth PL6 7PY
United Kingdom

British Library Cataloguing in Publication Information Available

**Library of Congress Cataloging-in-Publication Data**
Feinstein, Sheryl.
   Parenting the teenage brain : understanding a work in progress /
Sheryl Feinstein.
      p. cm.
   Includes bibliographical references and index.
   ISBN-13: 978-1-57886-620-5 (hardcover : alk. paper)
   ISBN-10: 1-57886-620-0 (hardcover : alk. paper)
   ISBN-13: 978-1-57886-621-2 (pbk. : alk. paper)
   ISBN-10: 1-57886-621-9 (pbk. : alk. paper)
   1. Parent and teenager. 2. Adolescent psychology. 3. Teenagers.
4. Parenting. I. Title.
   HQ799.15.F45 2007
   649'.125–dc22                                   2007002333

Manufactured in the United States of America.

To my four children,
James, Rachel, Scott, and Jennifer,
and my son-in-law, Christopher

# CONTENTS

# FOREWORD

This book is a pleasure to introduce. I am quite delighted to see this new book on parenting by Dr. Sheryl Feinstein. She has linked new and compelling research on the adolescent brain with the ever-challenging role of parenting. Dr. Feinstein's thought-provoking yet amusing discussion gives us a refreshing opportunity to deepen our understanding of the adolescent and to refine our parenting skills.

This book deals with everything from dating to driving to drugs. An abundance of practical advice, with a dash of groundbreaking research, is offered at every turn of the page. Much of it validates what we've already been doing as parents, and other parts shed new light on creating a more joyful ride through adolescence for the entire family. The real-life anecdotes included throughout the book add a sensibility and smile to the journey. We are given hope that through understanding, stamina, and patience we can raise healthy, happy, and successful teenagers.

One of the most impressive features of this book is its broad coverage of the challenges involved in parenting. Chapter 1 talks about the developing adolescent brain and how it differs from the child and adult brain. Chapters 2, 3, and 4 discuss general tactics that work or don't work with adolescents (don't nag, do communicate). Then chapters 5 through 10 go into specific issues families face with the social, emotional, physical, educational, and technological changes happening within and around adolescents. All of these chapters focus on practical suggestions for dealing with teenagers.

The final chapter examines at-risk teenagers with issues such as addiction, steroid use, and cutting, giving a healthy perspective to unhealthy choices. The family with an at-risk teenager is often smart to seek the support of a counselor, but the family also needs practical strategies for coping; this book supplies them. Finally, the book has a Parenting Glossary. Written in parent-friendly terms, it is a quick reference to everything from brain terminology to techno-expressions.

Those of us who have been involved in education and brain research welcome this informed application to parenting. Dr. Feinstein has certainly produced a significant and long-overdue book on parenting the teenage brain. I think you'll enjoy it.

Eric Jensen
Jensen Learning at www.jensenlearning.com
San Diego, California

# ACKNOWLEDGMENTS

I thank Sue Jordan for her continual support and expertise, Vicki Bachmayer for guiding me through the difficult moments and celebrating the best moments, and Jen Sharp for proofreading even when there was no time to proofread. Thanks to the Augustana College Computer Help Desk headed by Cheryl Swanson and to Judith Howard and Lisa Brunnick, who came to my rescue more than once, for library assistance.

I also express my appreciation to my colleagues in the Augustana Education Department, with special attention to Bob Kiner, Sharon Andrews, and Belinda Kaffar for their professional encouragement and collaboration. Thank you to Rachel Feinstein for patience and diligence with the index and to Karen Miller for her knowledge and skills. A special thank you to Lindsey Chaplin, Ryan and Colleen Jordan, Jamie and Amanda Gibbons, Shira Feinstein, and the Augustana Adolescent Development students for their continual inspiration. And last, but not least, I thank my parents, Jack and Phyllis Gibbons, for giving me a first-class education in parenting.

# ❶

# THE TEENAGE BRAIN: A WORK IN PROGRESS

Teenagers are perplexing, intriguing, and spirited creatures. In an attempt to discover the secrets to their thoughts and actions, parents have tried talking, cajoling, and begging them for answers. The result has usually been just more confusion, but new and exciting light is being shed on these veiled marauders. What was once thought to be hormones run amuck can now be explained with modern medical technology. Functional magnetic resonance imaging (fMRI) and positron emission tomography (PET) scans view the human brain while it is alive and functioning. Thanks to a group of dedicated neuroscientists, we can actually see which areas of the teenage brain are involved in various thought processes. To no one's surprise, the teenage brain is under heavy construction! These discoveries are helping parents understand the (until now) unexplainable teenager. Neuroscience can help parents adjust to the highs and lows of teenage behavior.

## PUTTING THE PUZZLE TOGETHER

Did you know . . .

- . . . teens are sculpting a brand-new brain?
- . . . parts of the brain increase in efficiency by 100 percent during adolescence?
- . . . teenagers and adults rely on different parts of the brain? Teen brains are ruled by emotion and adult brains by logic.
- . . . there will be over one thousand trillion (that's 1,000,000,000,000,000!) synaptic connections in the teen's brain by the end of adolescence?

Who is this straight-A student who leaves the homecoming lock-in dance because she feels "imprisoned"? Who is the middle-schooler who flies into a rage when, after four hours of playing on the Internet, is told by his parents it's time to do homework? This perplexing, moody, and sometimes defiant creature is someone adults have wrestled with themselves to understand for ages. But with new technology, we can look beyond hormones and growth spurts to the field of neuroscience for enlightenment. It isn't just bodies that are blooming during the teenage years—brains are also blossoming.

One of my favorite stories was shared by a woman about her own adolescence. She recalled how, as a young teen, her mother had taken her dress shopping for a family portrait. After hitting multiple stores, her mother insisted that she buy a dress that she absolutely hated. It looked like something her mother, or maybe even grandmother, would wear, and she thought she looked hideous in it. In spite of her pleading and whining, her mother simply refused to exchange the dress. So she did what any card-carrying, self-serving adolescent would do: she staged a burglary. First, she ransacked her home, then herself, and then the dress. She then called her mom to report the incident; this all seemed logical at the time. After an initial assessment of the scene by the mom, it was obvious that her daughter was fine and that nothing had been taken from the home. In fact, she noticed the only damage was to her daughter's dress. Upon this realization, her mother paused, stared straight at her daughter, and then started the conversation with a common parent mantra, "*What* were you thinking?!"

As a parent of four and an educator, I've witnessed firsthand the erratic and often incomprehensible behavior of adolescents. For example, my own high school junior just flew out the door on his way to get his early bird ID picture taken for school. This is a picture they wear for identification throughout the school year. James had greased his hair in a style reminiscent of Danny Zuko in *Grease* and had borrowed a pair of horn-rimmed glasses for the photo shoot. About a third of his class has decided to do something similar. The fact that they will wear these IDs for a full year never crosses their minds.

For many years I believed, as many parents still do, that all the inexplicable, often frustrating bad-boy behavior of teenagers had to do with puberty and maturity. After all, how many times have you heard the phrase "Hormones are raging"? Teens are children in adult bodies, puberty is striking, and they are too emotionally immature to handle it. And then in came the cavalry—neuroscientists from all over the world dressed in lab coats and equipped with fMRIs and PET scans collectively scrutinizing the most perplexing of entities, the teenager. Information began to pour in, and the pieces of the puzzle began to fall into place.

Scientists discovered that teenagers don't act or think like adults because their brains actually function in a different way. Teenage brains are, quite simply, a work in progress. Typically, this transformation is a prickly proposition for both teens and their families, but the trials and tribulations of adolescence give teenagers a second chance to develop and create their brain.

There are three major transformations that occur in the brain during the teenage years:

- Overproduction of dendrites and synaptic connections
- Pruning (use it or lose it)
- Myelination—the process of insulating the neurons and synaptic connections

## Overproduction

Sam had spent a busy day in school staring and sleeping; it was Friday night and he was now ready for some fun. He started with computer games—Madden 2006—and progressed on to Grand Theft Auto. Around 9:00 P.M. his good buddy Jeff called. "Hey, you wanna go out?" Sam's quick response was, "Sure that sounds great—where should we meet?" They settled on the local quick stop where they decided to buy toilet paper, lots of it. They then spent the evening teepeeing "friend's" houses. Little do these two boys realize that their life experiences are creating the brain they will take into adulthood.

In the brain, every new experience and bit of information creates a dendrite. Dendrites are small hairlike structures that emerge from neurons (the brain cells that are most closely linked to learning). Dendrites receive information from other neurons when they connect with their fellow neurons' axon. Every neuron has one axon that sends information and thousands of dendrites that receive information.

When neurons communicate with each other, synaptic connections are created and learning occurs. Learning a new vocabulary word, a dance step, or how to add fractions grows dendrites and builds synaptic connections. The more you engage in an activity, the more dendrites grow and the stronger the synaptic connections become. Adolescents are acquiring knowledge at an unprecedented rate. High school course requirements such as English composition, geometry, and biology all contribute to the growth of dendrites and the making of synaptic connections throughout the brain. Teens who spend their time reading and doing math are strengthening those areas of their brain. On the other hand, teens who spend time watching television or playing video games are strengthening those areas of their brain—they will become very good at playing video games.

Experience-related dendrites, synapses, and neural networks (knowledge) facilitate brain growth. Understanding from doing, applying, and practicing is a matter of cause (what we do) and effect (brain growth). The impact of experience on the brain can be seen in research that compared the dendrites of high school dropouts with college graduates. The college graduates had significantly more dendrites due to all the challenges and enrichment in their lives. During the teen years, there is a second opportunity to build a smarter, more efficient brain (the first chance was the preschool years).

Neuroscientists have discovered there is an overproduction of dendrites and synaptic connections during adolescence. By the end of adolescence, the brain contains more than 100 billion neurons and another 1,000 billion support cells. The 100 billion neurons form more than 1,000 trillion connections with each other—more than all of the Internet connections in the world. Academically, adolescence is a prime time to tap into a person's potential. Short-term memory increases by 30 percent during adolescence, which leads to increases in intelligence, reasoning, and problem-solving ability. Talented athletes and musicians also develop, strutting their stuff on the field or in the concert hall. (The difference in ability between the ninth-grade band, where the trumpet section ends a piece one measure behind everyone else, and the senior band that evokes emotion and demonstrates technique is palpable.)

Do these improvements mean that teens should spend all their time engaged in formal learning? Probably not. Still, at this critical time in development, the more time that is dedicated to reading, writing, math, music, and sports, the better the brain that is built.

## Pruning

This overproduction process is then followed by a reduction in information. That's right, you actually lose some of the stored data (this is not necessarily a bad thing). The brain works on the use-it-or-lose-it system. Information that is regularly used is deemed important and becomes stronger and easier to remember. Information that is not used is deemed unimportant and is forgotten, or pruned. (Students may forget the dates of all the battles that occurred during the Civil War, but they will remember what caused the Civil War and the important ramifications that occurred because of it.) In children and adults, about 1 to 2 percent of the brain is pruned each year. During adolescence, pruning happens on a massive scale, and about 15 percent of the synaptic connections are let go.

Every area of the teenage brain is pruned. A teen with a great deal of knowledge in one area will lose 15 percent of that stored information, although the bulk of it will remain intact. This may sound like troubling news, but in fact it is just the opposite; his brain is actually more efficient after discarding some of its inconsequential information. A teen, however, who has spent little time engaged in learning, will also lose 15 percent of her knowledge and she will be left with a sparse portion of information.

## Myelination

Twenty tenth-graders were chosen to be in a trial science class that encouraged real-world exploration and investigation. Students were chosen on the basis of their interest in science and a proven level of responsibility. About four weeks into class, the students were given the assignment of identifying various indigenous plants in a field located about ten miles away from the high school. The teacher gave them clear directions to the site, a list of necessary supplies, and the infamous teacher caution of "You are representing your school—act accordingly."

The next day twenty kids hopped into twenty cars (they all needed their own wheels) and headed for the field. For some unexplainable reason, on the drive there three of the boys started vying for the lead; before you knew it, their wild hair sprouted and all three boys were recklessly speeding down the highway. Faster and faster they went; they were sailing past traffic, laughing, and having a blast.

Ironically, and as fate would have it, two of the cars they passed on their wild and excellent adventure were a group of teachers from their high school on their way to lunch. Needless to say, the teachers did not miss a beat in identifying the culprits and reporting them to the principal. Clearly, savvy decision making (a result of myelination) had not been included in their list of supplies.

Finally, myelination occurs, which fine-tunes the brain. Myelin, a fatty substance that insulates neurons, allows for communication between areas of the brain to occur more efficiently and quickly. The frontal lobes, the section of the brain responsible for abstract thinking, good decision making, analyzing, and problem solving, are among the last parts to receive myelin (which is why we don't teach the formula for pi in math or Shakespeare's *Romeo and Juliet* until high school). As the frontal lobes mature during adolescence, the quality of thinking increases. Teenagers don't think more, so much as they think better. They become capable of understanding symbolism, thinking abstractly, and appreciating a more sophisticated sense of humor. Myelin increases communication up to one hundred times within the parts of the teenage brain. Eventually, teens are better able to remember information, think logically, evaluate, and find solutions than they were in childhood.

Adjusting to their new frontal lobe capabilities doesn't happen overnight. Disorganization and poor decision making are side effects of the transition from a childhood brain to an adult brain. The middle-schooler has a particularly difficult time getting organized. Organizing backpacks, completing homework, and finishing chores are all done in a haphazard manner, if at all. Parents should keep the word "tolerance" constantly in mind during their children's adolescence—and practice time management and study skills as appropriate antidotes.

## THREE OTHER CONSIDERATIONS

The three processes of overproduction, pruning, and myelination are not the only changes occurring in the teenage brain. Three other forces are at work:

- Teenagers relying on the emotional part of their brain
- Windows of opportunity
- Windows of sensitivity

Amy was an attractive, assertive, and confident senior. She didn't hesitate to raise her hand in a discussion (she was an active participant) or to correct her teachers and mother if she felt it was warranted (a mixed blessing).

One day Amy was late passing between classes and landed in AP English two minutes late. Her school had a strict tardy policy: late for class meant spending the class period in detention. Mr. Madison, the teacher said, "Amy you're late, head to detention."

Being a senior, Amy was more than aware of the tardy policy and she had seen more than a few of her friends tramp down the dreary halls toward detention. But for some reason, on this day, in this class, with this teacher, she was outraged. Instead of quietly leaving the area, she blew up. She said to Mr. Madison, "You were blocking the door, that's why I couldn't get in. I can't believe this! Why should I have to go to detention? It's not fair! It's just stupid to sit looking at a wall and have to miss class. This is your fault. I'm telling my mom!" The tirade continued for close to three minutes—it seemed longer to anyone listening.

Controlling her own emotions, taking responsibility for her actions, and getting along with others—at this moment in time, such skills were not evident in Amy's actions. Adults can want it for them, guide them, and support them, but ultimately the teenager has to do this on his or her own, which leads us to other changes in the teenage brain.

Teenagers actually rely on a different part of their brain than adults to interpret information. Adults use their frontal lobes, a logical, reflective part of the brain, to deduce meaning. Teenagers use the amygdala, the emotional center of the brain, to interpret that same information. The result of the overemphasis on emotions is a great deal of misunderstanding and misinterpreting of information. Reading body and facial language is something teens are in the process of learning. No wonder they interpret a peer's stares as "They don't like me." Worse still, they interpret a parent asking the innocuous question "Where are you going?" as a control freak, and they confront the parent with the angry and perhaps tearful accusation "You're trying to run my life!"

The teenage brain also represents a window of opportunity, a chance to learn something quickly and with more ease than at any other time of life.

We encounter such windows of opportunity throughout our lifespan; some are large windows and others are dramatically narrow. For instance, a foreign language is most easily learned before puberty, a strong argument for starting Spanish or Chinese in preschool or elementary school. Severe vision problems must be corrected before the age of two or blindness will continue for a lifetime. Babies need to bond with their parents for the first two years to be socially and emotionally healthy. Babies who are neglected or abused have attachment disorder issues and are at higher risk of school failure and engaging in criminal acts. These are all times when the brain is particularly sensitive to learning new information.

The windows of opportunity for the teenager are impulse control (learning how to curb their tempers), developing relationships (friends and mates), and expanding communication skills (hence their attraction to the phone). Never will it be easier for them to learn these skills and never are they more motivated to do so.

Adolescence also represents a window of sensitivity. If the brain is exposed to certain chemicals during this period of development, it will be more detrimental to its health than if it were exposed to them at other times. The big danger for teens is addiction. Never will addiction to alcohol, drugs, or smoking occur more quickly than during the teenage years. This is a double whammy, because they are also much more resistant to recovery. Chapter 11 covers addiction and other at-risk behaviors.

## OTHER CHANGES HAPPENING DURING ADOLESCENCE

Changes in the brain of the adolescent do not happen in isolation. It is during the teen years that a sense of identity is developed. Questions like "Am I a student? An athlete? A musician? Are my friends preppy or Goth? Should I be a Republican or Democrat? Am I Lutheran or Buddhist?" all lead to the big question of "Who am I?"

The search for identity is one of the most important jobs that teenagers have, and they pursue this mission with a vengeance. In order to discover an answer to this question, adolescents try on different hats, looking for the perfect fit. One morning parents wake up to a swing dancer and the next morning, a car freak. Society's expectations are generally high in this regard. By the end of high school, we expect them to have chosen a college, a vocational school, or a job; have a political stance; and have decided on a religious philosophy. This is a lot to require in a short span of time.

Seeking autonomy and separation from the family is also a normal part of growing up. Teenagers want to make their own decisions and form their own opinions. They want to choose their own
clothes, hairstyles, and friends. It's a difficult position they adopt,
trying to balance the desire to be distinctive while at the same time
conforming to the crowd. Teens need parents who will let them
make these decisions in slow increments. Too much freedom will
be construed as rejection, not enough as imprisonment. They want
to make choices and argue with adults, but they do not want complete freedom.

Last but not least, puberty strikes. Dramatic physical changes
occur in adolescent bodies. They suddenly grow six inches in six
months, are randomly sprinkled with acne, have budding breasts,
and hair everywhere. No wonder middle-schoolers feel uncomfortable in their own skins!

So now that we have an idea of what's going on in a teenager's
head, we can look at what this means for parents. Before reading
the rest of this book, take a few minutes to reflect on your own
teenage years. Reminisce about some of the things that were important to you during middle school and high school. Recall a few
decisions you made or fights you had with teachers or parents; list
things you might do differently if only you knew then what you
know now. Even talk to your parents about what it was like to raise
you—such a conversation can be very enlightening. (The mind can
be kind and diminish the struggles of our own adolescence, so getting your parents' perspective can be a reality check.)

For instance, Sarah was having trouble with her fourteen-year-
old daughter who did not hand in her homework. She happened to
mention this to her own mother and, much to her surprise, her
mother replied, "You did that all the time." Sarah had no recollection of that part of her past, and instead envisioned herself as always being a hard-working, studious youth. A dose of reflection on
our own adolescence helps create an atmosphere of empathy. This
is an important mental state for a parent to engage in when raising

teens and will help us assist them in this challenging passage in their lives.

## FAST FACTS

- Twelve- to thirteen-year-olds are substantially slower than adults at doing mental addition, memory, or simple motor skills.
- There is a great deal of difference between a young adolescent's brain and an older adolescent's brain.
- Pruning seems to curb attention deficit hyperactivity disorder (ADHD) symptoms and Tourette's syndrome—both conditions actually benefit from it.
- Disorders that most commonly appear during late adolescence, such as schizophrenia and obsessive-compulsive disorder (OCD), get worse with pruning.

**2**

# PARENTING STYLES: WHAT KIND OF PARENT ARE YOU?

During adolescence, brain changes occur at an unprecedented rate and parents are expected to accommodate and modify at every turn. Before long, we find ourselves dancing fast to a wild and wooly rumba without knowing any of the correct steps. This can be challenging—not to mention demoralizing—when the person we're trying to dance with seems to put the same energy into pushing away when we're trying to connect. Understanding the unique teenage brain helps us gauge how to influence and guide these restless souls.

## PUTTING THE PUZZLE TOGETHER

Did you know . . .

- . . . teens not only need but want structure from parents?
- . . . there is a preferred style of parenting for the teenage brain?
- . . . discussion is the best form of discipline for teenagers?

- . . . the vast majority of teens list at least one of their parents as being among the most important influences in their lives?

What do adolescents want from parents?

> For my mom it would be trust, she doesn't seem like she does. And chill out—my mom is more like tense, takes things so seriously.
> My dad believes in mistakes; he always gives me a second chance.
> Easy to talk with, not so overprotective. I'm not afraid of them.
> They ask me "Why?" a lot—I like that.
> To understand, and not be so strict.
> Trust and understand me more.

Despite intermittent clouds, storms, and hail, the outlook is sunny—teenagers genuinely believe parents matter. In fact, the majority of teens think highly of their parents and enjoy (yes, you read that correctly) spending time with them. This affirming information makes it easier for parents to maintain a hopeful equilibrium when dealing with sporadic teenage skirmishes.

Not only do they like us, but we matter when it comes to their mental, social, and emotional well-being. High-quality relationships between parents and teens are linked to better grades, fewer behavior problems, and higher academic expectations. The advantages don't stop there; positive parent/teen relationships are correlated with fewer violent behaviors and less delinquency, drug use, and sexual activity. Plus, these kids have the added bonus of getting along better with people outside the family: their peers and teachers. The verdict is clear—teens need parents.

## PARENTING STYLES

Style. Everybody's got one, from the model on the catwalk to the teenager gyrating at the school dance. When it comes to parenting, there are three main styles of raising kids: authoritative, authoritarian, and permissive. No parent exclusively uses one style and only one style, but one method does tend to dominate in a family.

These three parenting styles are not created equal. There is a general consensus among experts that one parenting method rises like cream to the top of the pitcher. This style is best suited to promote emotional stability and social responsibility while the others strip teens of self-esteem and confidence.

Take the following mini-quiz to get an indication of your parenting style. Circle the answer that is closest to your reaction. Find your answers and the parenting style that best describes you in Figure 2.1.

### Authoritative

Authoritative parents are democratic parents. In this egalitarian world, thoughts and opinions are taken into consideration by the majority (parents) and the minority (teens). Authoritative parents actually listen to their teens when making rules and decisions. The parents ultimately make the judgment because they have the adult cranium, but they keep in mind the needs and wants of all parties. No wonder teens thrive in this atmosphere—it's teenage-brain compatible. Their frontal lobes are ripe for decision making and communicating and they are just waiting for a chance to practice these tasks. Authoritative parents open the door and invite them to participate. Granted, their skills are a bit shaky at first, but they do improve.

Kids raised in these homes are encouraged to make their own decisions, to take responsibility, and to become autonomous. Of course, age-appropriate discretion is essential. A young teen is capable of making decisions about what clothes to wear to the mall; an older teen is better at deciding whom to date. While parents nurture all of this independence, they are also monitoring it. Teenage brains need adult brains lurking in the background, watching over and sheltering them. Parents need to know where

1. My teenager stays out thirty minutes beyond curfew without calling. I
   a. let it go
   b. ground her for a week
   c. talk about it to see what the reason is
2. My teenager needs to mow the lawn. I
   a. tell him it needs to be done sometime that day
   b. interrupt his phone call and say to do it now
   c. do it for him
3. My teenager wants to smoke cigarettes. I
   a. tell her no and that's the end of discussion
   b. buy her cigarettes
   c. talk to her about her views on this and ultimately say not in this
      house
4. My teenager doesn't clean his room. I
   a. clean it for him
   b. ignore the problem, but don't allow him to drag the mess into the
      rest of the house
   c. ground him until he cleans it up
5. My teenager is embarrassed to be seen with me.
   a. That's normal, and we respect it.
   b. That's ridiculous. We do things I think families should do together.
   c. Who cares? I'm busy anyway.

Answers:
Authoritative:    1. c, 2. a, 3. c, 4. b, 5. a
Authoritarian:    1. b, 2. b, 3. a, 4. c, 5. b
Permissive:       1. a, 2. c, 3. b, 4. a, 5. c

**Figure 2.1    Parenting Quiz**

their teens are, whom they are with, and what they are doing. The
authoritative parent is ever vigilant.

Authoritative parents accept the fact that teenagers can morph
from rebellious to pouting to compassionate in a nanosecond, and
somehow through it all realize that hidden behind that perplexing
exterior is a great kid. They appreciate the fact that, in spite of

some fairly inappropriate behavior, teenagers sparkle with optimism, love a spirited conversation, and can electrify a room with their enthusiasm. They then go the extra step of letting their teen know that they like them. This creates a warm and caring landscape for teenagers to sprout and spread their wings. This haven of acceptance is a lifeline to the teenager, because the outside world can be a harsh and unfriendly place.

The most frequent form of discipline used in these homes is talking about the problem. Researchers back this strategy; countless studies have found that discussion is the best form of discipline for teens (and by discussion I don't mean lecture—more about this in chapter 3). Teenagers' brains are equipped to express their thoughts and understand ours. When punishment is used—sometimes there is no getting around it—these parents opt for grounding or time out, rather than physical punishment.

The advantages of the authoritative parenting style for the teen is enormous. Teens benefit with more social competence and fewer psychological and behavioral problems. They have better grades, are more self-reliant, less anxious, less depressed, and less likely to be delinquent. They have better-rounded peer groups because they tend to gravitate to groups that admire both adult and youth values. These advantages hold for all ethnic groups, socioeconomic backgrounds, and traditional and nontraditional families.

All experts agree this is the desired parenting style. In fact, this style is so preferable that researchers advocate that having even one parent who is authoritative when the other parent is permissive or authoritarian in a family is preferable to both parents being authoritarian or permissive. In this case, consistency is not the dominating factor. A round of applause for authoritative parents!

## Authoritarian

This story came tumbling out of the mouth of a nineteen-year-old: "My dad is so strict, we all hate him. My younger sister, Danielle, is sixteen. We all knew she had a boyfriend, even Mom, but nobody would tell Dad. He listened in on Danielle's phone call and heard her boyfriend say 'I love you,' then she heard Dad hang up the phone. She called me right away and said, 'How soon can you come home?' He freaked out and started in on her right away. He said things like 'This is disgusting,' 'You'll be pregnant and married before you get out of high school.'"

The slogan of authoritarian parents is "My way or the highway." Authoritarian parents allow no independence of body, mind, or spirit in the house. Instead, they value obedience and submission. These parents are inflexible rulers who want their children to fit into a mold specifically designed by them rather than for their offspring.

As might be expected, this parenting style is fraught with problems. A relationship based on control, control, control is bound to be a lose/lose proposition. Teens raised in such households lack confidence, have more social problems, and have difficulty getting along with their peers and teachers. Their emotional and social problems probably stem from insecurity; after all, their thoughts and opinions are bludgeoned at home and they never learned how to negotiate within the safer family setting.

When issues arise, authoritarian parents make all the decisions, with no input from the teenager. For instance, one middle-schooler was removed from the football team because his mother found out, by looking at a computerized report generated by the school, he was currently receiving a D in social studies. When he tried to explain it was because the teacher had not yet entered his grades from when he was sick and that he was actually earning a B in the class, he was met with no room for discussion and told he was off the team. He thought (reasonably) that this was unfair and the stage was set for rebellion.

If practice makes perfect, then these kids are in trouble because they get no practice making decisions. Not only does this make for an unsatisfactory home life, but the real world becomes scary for them. They feel insecure about coming up with age-appropriate solutions to problems they encounter in school or with friends. Not surprisingly, these teens have more trouble independently solving problems and making decisions—important life skills. And that's just the beginning of their difficulty.

There is no feeling of warmth or acceptance in their house. Authoritarian parents are strict disciplinarians who stress rigid adherence to the house rules. When the teen dares to question the rules, he or she is met with by the brick walls of "because I said so" and "case closed." Many of these parents do not hesitate to inflict physical punishment. The result of harsh and physical punishment on the teen extends beyond the family. Teenagers tend to model this violence outside the home in their other relationships. This provides a definite obstacle to getting along with others. In certain ways these parents are indoctrinating their teens to follow and not lead in the adult workforce. The consequences are far-reaching.

This type of parenting creates a combination of rebellion and dependency in the teenager. They are more hostile to their parents; they resent their control and domination. The weaker ones remain codependent and the stronger ones rebel. Perhaps that explains why they have a higher rate of promiscuity than teenagers with authoritative parents. This is not a recipe for raising healthy adolescents.

## Permissive

Permissive parents come in two forms: indulgent and neglectful. Both share the common bond of inconsistency. Sometimes they are active, connected forces in their child's life, and sometimes not.

An extreme example of permissive parenting comes from a family I knew during high school. Allison was from a permissive home that combined both indulgent and neglectful parenting. Her parents were some of the wealthiest and most unconventional in the Midwest. One evening in tenth grade I received a phone call from

Allison's parents saying they hadn't seen her in a couple of days (most parents would have been hysterical within twenty-four hours) and asking if I knew where she was. I didn't know and told them so, which ended the conversation. Her mother's telephone search continued.

On the third day of her hiatus, Allison phoned her parents to inform them that she had gone with a band to New Orleans for Mardi Gras. A bit shaken and greatly relieved, her parents immediately retrieved her, but with no reprimands, no chastising, not a word of disappointment. You'd think she had never been gone. Many people would assume that Allison would have been relieved that her parents hadn't met her in a state of hysteria, ready to send her to boarding school or at least lock her in her room for the next year. Instead, when I was complaining to her one night about my parents' tyrannical, absolutely unfair rules, she murmured that she wished she had a curfew like I did because she felt her parents didn't care. Teenagers do get it.

Overindulgent parents express their love by giving into their kid's every demand. The children make the decisions and the parents ante up. (I know of a case in which the parents surrendered the master bedroom because their son needed more space.) Because the amygdala is in charge of the teenage brain, household decisions seem to be sparse on logic and heavy on pleasure. And with no adult brain to temper the situation, things quickly get out of hand. Permissive parents often want friendship from their teen, so they act more like peers than parents. You've all seen the mother with the belly ring who offers all the kids a beer. Kids have lots of friends but only one set of parents. Be a parent, not a friend.

On the positive side, teens with indulgent parents have high levels of self-confidence. It's no wonder they feel good about themselves—the universe essentially revolves around them! But because of the lack of monitoring, they also have more substance abuse, more misbehavior, and less engagement in school. They are not ready to make all of their own decisions; parental guidance is a requirement for nourishing teenagers.

Neglectful parents send a clear message that they do not care about their kids. These are the parents who never attend their teens' activities, are not at home for dinner, and generally have an "I couldn't care less" attitude. Youths with neglectful parents are the least socially competent and have the most psychological and behavioral problems. These teens naturally gravitate to their peers for a sense of belonging. This is a problem, a big problem. In general, peer groups tend to stress fun and partying. In moderation this is fine, but when it's the only message teens get, it's difficult for them to find a balance between fun and responsibility. In both the overindulgent and neglectful homes of permissive parents, teens receive little guidance. They aren't stupid; they interpret lax discipline as rejection. They may become domineering and self-centered, but without limits, they also feel insecure.

## FAST FACTS

- More than four in five teenagers (84 percent) agreed or strongly agreed with the statement that they think highly of their mother.
- More than half of teenagers (57 percent) want to be like their mother.
- More than three-quarters of teenagers (79 percent) enjoy spending time with their mother.
- Eighty-nine percent think highly of their father.
- Sixty-one percent want to be like their father.
- Seventy-six percent enjoy spending time with their father.

**③**

# STRATEGIES THAT WORK AND DON'T WORK WITH TEENAGERS

Flashes of anger and mean-spirited comments, or empathetic gestures and social activism—a parent of a teenager can never be sure whether Dr. Jekyll or Mr. Hyde will sit down at the breakfast table each day. The teenage brain is on an express train that seems to go nowhere.

## PUTTING THE PUZZLE TOGETHER

Did you know . . .

- . . . sometimes it's okay to let teenagers have the last word in an argument?
- . . . adolescents talk more to their moms than their dads and ask for more advice from mom?
- . . . teens need a great deal of love and affection from both parents?
- . . . mothers consistently underestimate the stress their teenagers face?

Teenagers yearn for self-control but frequently come up short. In spite of this disagreeable adolescent behavior, parents who are able to summon the energy to explain decisions and even include the teen in the decision-making process have an easier journey and foster happier and healthier kids. What worked well with the elementary school child will not fly with the teen. Why should it? Their brains are equipped to understand more and they crave the conversation.

## WHAT DOES NOT WORK

### Lecture

No matter what your chosen parenting style, certain techniques do not work. Lecturing, a parental favorite, fits neatly into this category. As a parent, it is all too tempting to launch into a trusty lecture and begin imparting valuable information to the teenager. After all, as adults we have survived adolescence, possess a broader life perspective (I easily have twenty to thirty years on my children), and have knowledge that could make their lives easier. If they would just listen to us, they wouldn't have to endure the struggles and disappointment we did when growing up.

I was recently in this very situation with my youngest son. As a parent, I am fully aware of the value of studying in school—drop out and you'll end up in poverty. This information could save my son pain and heartache and surely could make him want to study harder in school, right? With the best of intentions, the lecture begins. Unfortunately, no one is listening.

Body language is your first clue that you've lost your audience: teens roll their eyes and shake their heads like they cannot believe you just said that. You find yourself repeating the question "Are you listening to me?" and making the old demand "Look at me when I talk to you."

## Nagging

Nagging is another technique that just doesn't work. Some parents are under the misguided notion that if they say something over and over again it will eventually sink into their teen's brain. Perhaps the teen will even thank them for pestering them to the point of taking action. Unfortunately, kids tend to tune out or become aggravated with the nagger.

I asked one teenage girl if her parents ever nagged her. She was quick to answer, "Oh yes, my mom always nags be about my messy room. She reminds me all the time to get in there; she says it looks like a tornado went through." She laughed at the image and gave her mother credit at least for being clever. I then asked her if the nagging worked and in all seriousness she said, "No. I still have a messy room. She doesn't understand I'm too busy talking on the phone to clean." I couldn't help but wonder if her mother would find her daughter's logic confusing or amusing.

## Timing

Another lose/lose scenario is spontaneously bringing up a subject that you feel is important, regardless of what the teen is currently doing. Interrupting them when they are already engaged in an activity is a surefire recipe for fireworks.

Let's say you just received a report card and it's evident that there is trouble brewing in chemistry. You say to your teenager, "Right here, right now, we're going to discuss your chemistry grades." Let's say that at this moment your teenager is busy instant messaging friends. Your conversation is not only bothering your teen during important social time, but interrupting him or her with something unpleasant as well. No wonder your comments are met with an irritated gnashing of their teeth, a glare, and probably, if pushed, an inappropriate word. Face it—if roles were reversed, you wouldn't like it either. For me, it's like being told to do the dishes right in the middle of watching *Gone with the Wind.*

A more effective approach is to tell them you want to talk about something that is important, like their chemistry grades, and then set up a time that works for all parties. Let them know what you want to talk about and then agree on a good time to talk. Showing them the same courtesy you would expect from others sets the stage for a positive discussion.

## Arguing

Arguing with a teen is pointless. They have energy, lots and lots of energy—more energy than we do—and too often are ready to take up the challenge. Because a parent and a teen rely on different parts of the brain to communicate (the frontal lobes and amygdala, respectively), both parties are easily frustrated. Parents get upset because teens don't think and speak like an adult; teens get upset because parents don't tolerate the emotional volcano inside them waiting to erupt.

Instead of arguing, say what you need to in a direct and succinct manner and then leave the room. It's just three steps: 1) Say your piece, 2) turn, and 3) go. As you leave the room, don't be surprised to hear one last word flung in your direction ("I hate you" or "You are so unfair")—just ignore it. Don't engage in a power struggle. Teens need the last word more than we do, so don't insist on having it. As frustrating as this advice may be, it can save everyone a lot of heartache. It's best to deal with a teenage brain by using the adult brain.

## Guilt and Personal Attacks

Ruling with guilt, withholding love, and making personal attacks is psychologically detrimental to the teen. Even if teenagers use these techniques on you all the time, you shouldn't respond in kind. Comments like "I hate you," "You're the worst mother ever," and "Everyone else gets to stay out until midnight" are just frequent mutterings of the adolescent. It isn't okay that teens approach conflict in this manner, but remember that they are a work in progress. As adults we know better, so we need to set the better example. When adults resort to such mean-spirited behavior, the ramifications for teens are serious. Adults who do so demonstrate to teens that their adolescent need for love and security are not met. Unkind words contribute to unhealthy development almost as much as does physical abuse. The father who calls his son a loser or his daughter a slut cuts deep. Depression and antisocial behavior are the remnants of such psychological abuse.

## WHAT DOES WORK

So what does work with teenagers? First and foremost, teenagers need unconditional love from their parents. They need to know you care about them and accept them (although you do not have to approve of everything they do). Teens need to know that their parents will stand beside them and help them when times get rough—and this message needs to be conveyed explicitly by our actions. Setting high expectations, establishing rules, and exhibiting tolerance are a powerful combination that parents can bring to the table.

### Communication

Expressing love and support starts with listening and communicating. The best way to help teenagers gain the trust of their parents is through conversation. Unfortunately, this is not always an easy proposition. Communication skills deteriorate during the teen years. Teens provide less information and what they do say is often colored with attitude. Teenagers have a triple disadvantage on the communication circuit—they misread emotions, their emotional amygdala is in power, and their prefrontal cortex is in an underdeveloped state. Parents with good communication skills can set a good example for the teenager to follow, or at least mollify an obstinate conversation.

There's good new and bad news when it comes to communicating with the teenage brain. First the bad news: because of all the changes going on in the teenage brain, adolescents often misinterpret body language and the spoken word. Deborah Yurgelun-Todd conducted compelling research on the teenage brain. Adults and teens were given the same photograph to view—a picture of a woman with fear on her face. All of the adults in the study correctly identified the emotion as fear, but only 50 percent of the teens identified fear as the emotion. Instead, they suggested the woman showed shock or surprise.

Curious about these findings, Yurgelun-Todd expanded the research in hopes of discovering the reason for the differing responses. She repeated the experiment but added fMRI scans on participants as they viewed the picture. She found that all of the adults used their frontal lobe, the part of the brain used for well-thought-out decisions and analyzing, when they interpreted the picture. The teens, on the other hand, used their amygdala, the emotional center of the brain. No wonder their responses were different—their brains function differently!

These results explain why teens make so many misinterpretations and misunderstandings: they rely on an emotional part of their brain to interpret body language. Researchers surmise that interpreting body language is a learned skill; it's not something we inherit. Teens are in the process of learning what the smirk, the shrug, and the stare mean.

How does this play out in real life? When a parent stares at teens while waiting for an answer, the teen interprets it as though the parent is furious. In the school lunchroom, a girl across the room turns her head in the other direction and another teen interprets it as a signal that no one else is welcome at the table.

Even adults sometimes revert back to using this part of the brain, particularly under stress. The upset father whose son is picked up for drunk driving may misread a colleague's comment or stare as a criticism of his work or life.

In the teen, the amygdala, not the frontal lobes, is in charge, which makes conversations potentially volatile. A calm comment is met with a storm of verbal abuse. An innocent question, such as "Are you wearing that shirt?" sets off a stream of tears and foot stomping, as a teenager bawls in response, "You think I'm fat. I hate you!" Because adolescents are such emotional communicators, it is easy to make light of their problems.

When you converse with your teen, it is important to respect her ideas, even when they seem trivial. I remember one mother telling how she had spent hours with her middle-school daughter as the daughter complained about how awful it was to have physical education—not to mention the required showers—first period of the day, because the teen's carefully coiffed hair and makeup were ruined. As an adult, she wanted to say that her daughter looked fine, to just put her hair in a ponytail and call it a day, and to assure her that all the other girls were too concerned with their own bodies to look at her in the showers. Parents want to express these perfectly clear and logical thoughts but, trust me, it's not what teens want to hear. Just listen and maybe even commiserate with comments like "I would hate to have gym first period" to let her know that you understand. Do not trivialize their concerns—at this point in their life, these are major worries!

One mother learned the power of listening the hard way. She recalled listening to her oldest daughter, Kristin, complaining and complaining about a middle-school teacher. She found herself saying things like "Maybe she's just trying to make sure all the kids do their best work" and "You need to listen to her instead of being mouthy." In essence, she constantly defended the teacher to try to make Kristin understand that there were two sides to the story; she did what she thought was her parental job. When she related her experience to a group of friends, one said, "There comes a time when they just want you to listen." What a difference this made! The tension between mother and daughter was totally diffused when the mother began to just listen and responded with comments like "That sounds very frustrating." Without expressing any disrespect toward the teacher, she still validated her daughter's feelings.

Luckily for parents, once the frontal lobes become fully functional, teens are able to think at a new and higher level. They learn to analyze, problem solve, and deduct. Their language skills increase at mind-boggling rates and they begin to understand symbolism, irony, and sarcasm. All these capabilities are exciting and wonderful, but for parents it may take some getting used to them. When a small child talks to a parent about a problem, the child is grateful when the parent provides a solution. The teen, on the other hand, doesn't necessarily want an answer to his or her discontent; teens want to be the ones who solve the problem while another person listens to them work it out. The following are communication tips for conversing with teens:

- Listen to him more than talk to him.
- Begin statements with "I" instead of "you" to diminish defensiveness.
- Be open to learning from your teenager and let him instruct you sometimes.
- Stay focused on her conversation and resist the temptation to interrupt with your own stories.
- Accept his opinions and ideas even when they differ radically from yours.
- Be an active listener and periodically ask questions to show interest.
- Match your emotional state to hers (unless it is hostile). If she is down, don't try to perk her up with bubbly optimism.
- Show empathy and identify with his point of view.

- Withhold advice unless she asks you for it (the less you offer, the more she'll ask).
- Allow him to discuss whatever topic he wishes.
- Think before you speak, especially if you are discussing a sensitive issue.
- Be pleasant and stay positive or else walk away.
- Avoid generalizations.
- Ask questions that require more than a one-word response.

So what are some good talking points for that much-awaited chat with your adolescent? Here are a few thoughts from teenagers:

> I like talking sports with my dad. He's the high school baseball coach and I'm on the team.
> We talk about school and my friends.
> My mom and I talk about my future—what I will be in life. I love singing and my mom said when I get older I should be in *American Idol*.

Topics about favorite classes, news about friends, movies, and politics all seem to be safe territory. Tread lightly and experiment a little to find out what topics your teen seems to enjoy talking about, and in general stay away from touchy issues. Every teen has different hot-button issues and, fortunately or unfortunately, it takes minimal probing to discover them. Without exception, every teenage girl I spoke to hated talking to her parents about boys. As one girl said, "It usually results in a lecture on how I'm too young, there's plenty of time for boys later." One girl, who felt her mom was being too persistent, said, "I told my mom it's my personal life, but she said I have no personal life—I'm her daughter. I wondered then, do I have no right to even write in a diary?" Of course, parents would love to have these conversations about the opposite sex, but if we hope to be included we need to listen to what our teenagers say and not jump to judgment.

Last but not least, find a good place to talk. A conversational setting can make a difference. Going out for ice cream or to dinner sets the stage for a pleasant talk. Going for a drive in the car—a popular retreat for adolescents—can set a tone of conciliatory fun. Besides being neutral territory, you have a captive audience and nobody has to face the other, which may lend a level of comfort to the conversation. (But remember, neither you nor your child can walk out on this conversation, so choose your words wisely!)

## Be a Source of Support

Teens need to know that they can rely on their parents when the going gets rough. They are naturally drawn to risky behavior and are unable to make good decisions, so you are guaranteed they will need a safety net at some point in time.

Consider, for instance, Matt and Bill, two teens who were caught with pot in the 1970s. If two boys ever needed their parents, it was these two—they faced serious legal charges that could very likely have landed them in juvenile correctional facilities. Both families were upset as the boys were taken to court for their first hearing. As they were leaving the courtroom, Matt's father leaned over and said, "I know you're a good kid. Stick by me and we'll get through this." Matt's dad sent him two messages with one statement: 1) "I'm going to help you get through this," and 2) "You need to listen to me."

The other boy, Bill, had had an erratic home life. His father had passed away and his mother was an overworked and underskilled parent. Bill received no guidance or support. He was punished and then left to fend for himself.

The difference in support between these two families made a dramatic difference in the lives of two boys. Matt is now an upstanding, middle-aged adult who has started several service organizations. He is a model citizen. Bill continued abusing drugs and ultimately died of an overdose.

Stick with your teen through difficult times so that a bad decision made during adolescence doesn't haunt him in his adult life. This is not the same as being permissive or enforcing no consequences for errant behavior. Parents can deliver consequences while still being supportive.

### Encourage Autonomy

Encourage independent thinking. Although this sounds simple, it is sometimes more difficult than you expect. After all, parents make all the decisions regarding religion, school, and friends for their younger children and it works just fine. When those children hit adolescence, suddenly the decisions parents make are not appreciated by the teenager. What's going on?

Building autonomy, a major job during adolescence, is what's going on. Adolescence is a time to explore and seek self-sufficiency. Teens are in the process of developing new interests, values, and goals. They want to establish an individual identity while maintaining connectedness with parents. Parents should expect to be baffled by some of the choices their son or daughter makes. It's not uncommon to see a president of the Young Republicans raised by a family of staunch Democrats or a straight-A student date a boy who is seriously contemplating dropping out of school. It's a mini-rebellion, albeit within the parameters of normal. Kids who are allowed or even encouraged by their parents to think for themselves tend to be more confident and better problem solvers.

Gradually, give your teens more freedom—start small and, as they prove themselves, loosen the reins a bit. Let young teens stay home alone for an evening during the school week. If they handle themselves appropriately, let them stay alone for longer periods of time. Take them to the mall with you, then take them to the mall but go your separate ways, and then set them free to go to the mall on their own. Teens are quick to identify and appreciate their newfound freedoms. "I can stay out later than before. You get more responsibility, more trust, but Mom checks up on me." And, "I get to stay out later, and get to stay home alone more. They trust me."

## Trust

Trust teenagers. Research has found that the more teens talk to their parents, the more their parents trust them. Although it is ultimately the teen's decision whether or not to talk to parents, encouraging communication falls under the parental parameters.

Most teens believe they should be trusted until they do something that shrouds them in suspicion. Examples of parental distrust can be found in such acts as opening their mail, reading a diary, searching their room, listening in on telephone conversations, or monitoring computer use. (Interestingly, parents—especially women—who were promiscuous in their own teenage years tend to be the ones who show mistrust of their teenage children without provocation.) Weigh heavily the potential consequences to your relationship with your teenager before showing your mistrust. Once trust between you has been breached, there is often damage to your mutual respect and your teen's behavior. Teens often interpret mistrust as a parent thinking that they are bad, so why bother being good? Don't let fear of showing mistrust lead you to turn a blind eye to real issues of concern, however; strive to achieve balance between trust and surveillance.

## Monitoring

You don't need a scientist to observe that decisions made by adolescents are not always the best ones. They streak at football games, cheat on tests, and drive recklessly. The advantages of a supervising adult brain staying in close proximity to a budding teenage brain are obvious. This is where monitoring comes into play. Monitoring means keeping track of your teen. It means knowing the answer to the question "It's 10:00. Do you know where your child is?" Successful parents know what their teens do, where they go, and with whom. Parents who monitor take a genuine interest in their kid's activities, know their friends, and know where they hang out.

Still, it's not always easy to monitor teens. Not only can teens be uncommunicative, but adults have busy, complicated lives, too. Time, jobs, aging parents, marriage, and illness are all barriers to monitoring. That being said, the benefits to the teenager and the family make monitoring worth the effort. Teens are less likely to get into trouble if they believe that their parents will find out about it. Teenagers who are monitored are less likely to lie, cheat, steal, engage in sexual behavior, or use drugs.

To be a good monitor, you need to know four things: 1) whom your teen is with, 2) where your teen is going, 3) what your teen plans to do, and 4) when your teen will be home. You also need to learn these things without a conversation becoming an interrogation, so stay in touch. Encourage teens to call home if they are going to be late. If they are late for curfew and you receive no call from them, call them yourself (waiting fifteen to twenty minutes is a reasonable amount of time). But don't be too helpful. One well-intentioned dad made a practice of calling to remind his son to return home ten minutes before curfew, and subsequently missed the teachable moment. A curfew is set not only to ensure a teen's safety in returning home but also to help build personal responsibility. Make teens responsible for keeping their end of the curfew bargain.

Also set a good example yourself. When you go out, tell your teens where you're going, when you'll be back, and how you can be reached. Start the habit of keeping a family calendar in early adolescence and encourage teens to keep one for themselves, too. By tenth grade, make teens primarily responsible for keeping track of their own activities. (Of course, an occasional reminder for a special event or responsibility is a courtesy everyone appreciates.)

Realize, too, that there is a big difference between *monitoring* a teen's thoughts and *controlling* a teen's thoughts. Don't get caught up in controlling your teen—trying to control her thoughts will not control her actions. Parents who focus on monitoring their teen's behavior and not monitoring his or her thoughts do the best. When teens become delinquent, there is usually a tendency to focus more on the psychological and less on the behavior, which creates a cycle of bad behavior. A teen who repeatedly breaks curfew by hours is better off having the car taken away for two days (managing his behavior) than by being yelled at with guilt-laden comments such as "Your mother was worried sick! She couldn't sleep, so now she'll be tired at work tomorrow" (employing psychological tactics).

A good solution is to encourage your teenager's involvement in adult-supervised activities, such as tennis lessons, the Key Club, or playing the clarinet. Make your home available and inviting to your teen and his friends. A parent who welcomes adolescents into his home, however loud and rowdy they may be, has the chance to supervise them. Make sure, however, to give teens space when they are there—no one likes to feel as if he or she were living with a secret agent who scrutinizes every move.

### Rules and Consequences

I once asked a group of teens for a list of their house rules and was surprised at the consistency of their responses.

Do my homework first.
  Homework first, then the computer.
  You can't go anywhere until you clean your room.
  No fighting in the house.
  I can't talk for over two hours on the phone. If she tells me more than twice, I lose my phone privileges. [Two hours seemed like a lot to me, but she assured me it was reasonable.]

Include teens in the process of making rules and consequences. Giving them input into the rules helps diffuse the emotion between both parties when rules are broken. One woman with two teenage boys related her insightful story: The older son was constantly grounded for breaking curfew by being ten to fifteen minutes late. Because his parents wouldn't tolerate this carelessness, there was constant warfare in the house. When the younger boy came of age, they discussed curfew with him. When they realized that all the other kids were allowed to stay out about half an hour later, they extended his curfew and the problem never surfaced. Yes, sometimes the solution is this easy.

Some of the consequences—positive and negative—that matter to teens are:

- Discuss, discuss, discuss. (This really is the best way to deal with teenage issues.)
- Natural consequences: "If you want your laundry done, put it in the hamper."
- Grandma's rule: Eat your peas and you can have dessert— "Turn in all your homework this week and you can stay out one hour later on Friday night."
- Telephone and computer use—restricting or increasing privileges.
- Grounding.
- Money—giving it or taking it away.
- Car—limit, eliminate, or extend its use.
- Spending time with your teen—even when he says he isn't interested, he often is.

The biggest mistake parents make is believing they have lost total control if a teenager breaks one rule. Going ballistic and imposing harsh punishments over a single infraction just lays the groundwork for a contentious relationship. Often parents get set in their ways and rules and find themselves in a never-ending power struggle with a teenager before they even know what is happening. Be sure to set clear guidelines, but be prepared to accept the fact that, even with your best efforts, you will encounter multiple misunderstandings. And then move on.

## Fun

I like to go shopping, to a football game, or eat Mexican food with my parents.
Go to movies.
I like to watch my step-dad play soccer and then we all play at the park.

Have fun with your teen. Too often this potential path to happy parenting is put on a back burner. If you are unsure about how to have fun with a teenager, put his or her interests first. Go to a place of his choosing, somewhere he is going to enjoy. Go shopping and resist the temptation to try on that little sweater from the career wear store. I know of one dad who took his son and a few of his friends to a Nine Inch Nails concert (that is defined as going the extra mile in my book). But does this mean that you always go wherever they want, whenever they want? No—it's a two-way street. Teens need to learn new things, too.

If they are going through a stage where they don't want their friends to see them with you, respect that. One girl actually tried to hide behind a pole at the movies when she saw her peers walking toward her mother and her. In this case, find a time and place where they are sure not to be seen. Family vacations can be a great retreat, with no chance of running into friends. For more discussion of this issue, look to the chapter 9 section "Teenagers Embarrassed to Be Seen with Family."

One warning: If every time you take them shopping, out to eat, or to a ballgame you end up beginning a discussion on a sensitive subject, the teen will quickly pick up on your not-so-subtle tactics and refuse to go. No one likes a surprise attack.

## Coping Skills

Life has many pitfalls and teens need to learn how to deal with its ups and downs in an appropriate manner. Teach them good coping skills. Teens who don't learn appropriate coping skills now may turn to drugs and alcohol instead; teens who rely on drugs and alcohol to cope have a very difficult time learning other strategies later in life. Setting a good example as a parent is fairly straightforward: When you are stressed announce, "I'm mad, so I think I'll go for a walk to clear my head." Hearing the words and seeing your example gives teens options for how to handle their own moments of crisis when they arise.

Encourage these coping skills for teens:

- Spend time with family and friends
- Join an extracurricular activity
- You
- Write in a journal
- Exercise
- Read books or magazines that make you feel good
- Don't watch the news for a month (it can be depressing)
- Talk to someone about your feelings (family, friend, or a counselor)
- Avoid stressful relationships

### School Involvement

The importance of parental involvement in school cannot be overemphasized. Teens whose parents are involved in school have better grades, are more motivated, and get along better with teachers and peers.

What is meant by school involvement?

- Support learning at home—For example, check in daily with a middle-schooler to see if homework is done. Hopefully, she can quickly be weaned from your reminders and take on this responsibility herself. Another example is to talk to teens about their teachers and school and provide help with home-work as needed.

- Communicate—Do your part to learn what is happening at school, during class and afterwards. Go to conferences, read newsletters, attend open houses, and respond to e-mails or phone calls. Talk to teachers, administrators, or counselors if you have a concern.
- Volunteer—Volunteer for fund-raisers, sign up for the Booster Club, or help pass out band uniforms. Join the PTA or other parent groups to help set policy and support extracurricular activities. Check with your teenager before your chaperone a school function and follow his or her wishes.

## FAST FACTS

- A mother's education level is the greatest indicator of a teenager's future success.
- The vast majority of teenage homicide is against their mother's abuser.
- Mothers who were promiscuous as teenagers are the least trusting of their own teenagers.
- Teenage girls have similar attitudes to sex and drugs as their mothers, whether their mothers openly talk about the subject or not.
- Parents matter! You play one of the most important roles in their academic success, motivation, and ability to get along with others.
- Families who have five meals together a week have teenagers who are more motivated to succeed and less likely to engage in drugs.

**4**

# TRIGGERING MISBEHAVIOR

When I was a boy of fourteen, my father was so ignorant I could hardly stand to have the old man around. But when I got to be twenty-one, I was astonished at how much he had learned in seven years.

—Mark Twain, "Old Times on the Mississippi,"
*Atlantic Monthly*, 1874

**W**hy is it that the same fourteen-year-old who can give you a complex, sophisticated, logical argument for staying out later than curfew nonetheless looks perplexed when you ask him what he is doing tonight? Neuroscience has shown that emotions rule in the teenage brain. Teens are just learning how to negotiate and balance between emotion and logic, and until the frontal lobes are under control, tensions and struggles in the home are almost guaranteed.

## PUTTING THE PUZZLE TOGETHER

Did you know . . .

- . . . younger adolescents say one thing and then do another?

- . . . older adolescents enjoy being active in their community?
- . . . teenagers interpret information differently than adults?
- . . . body language interpretation skills are learned during adolescence?

Mary was the mother of three girls. Her two oldest girls had finally reached young adulthood and, to her pride (and relief), they were doing very well. Mary had survived the tears, the flashes of temper, and the muddled thinking and was now looking forward to a calm and quiet future with her youngest daughter, Betsy. Through the storms and rages of the older girls' teen years, Betsy had remained sweet, caring, and loving toward her mother—a bastion of peace and calm. In fact, at age ten, Betsy had even promised her mother that she would never act like the older girls when she reached their age.

Unfortunately, this was not a binding contract.

As her youngest daughter approached her teenager years, the squabbles began. After one small skirmish, Mary accepted the fact that Betsy would follow in her sister's footsteps. In desperation, as Betsy stomped up to her room and slammed the door, Mary actually found herself yelling (pleading?), "But you promised!"

## ACCEPTING THE CHANGE

One of the primary reasons for tension between teens and their parents is the difference between rearing children and raising teenagers. Parents have a difficult time accepting the changes and increased abilities in teenage thinking. The tremendous growth, pruning, and other changes occurring in the brain contribute to the changing needs and behaviors of adolescents. It's not easy to lose the compliant child who hung on your every word, who looked at you as the font of all knowledge, and who is now replaced by a mutinous, fickle teenager.

Expecting the adolescent to forever remain a child sets you up for disappointment and disillusionment, for hurt and disappointment.

The parent who continues to treat a teenager as a child will meet re-bellion at every turn. Accepting the fact that the child-parent rela-tionship is over and embracing that different but potentially won-derful one that lies ahead is a giant leap toward getting along with a teenager.

As teens become more independent and outspoken, some par-ents feel like they are losing their child and they mourn or resent the transition. Rest assured—you are not losing your child. Rather, you're gaining a teenager. Some distancing from the family is a normal part of development. Teens no longer want to spend the majority of their time playing and relaxing with Mom and Dad. In-stead, they want to explore the world. This newfound indepen-dence is a sign of maturity, not a lack of love. Teenagers still need the support and love of the family. They desire to establish roots and spread their wings.

As discussed in chapter 2, teens don't want a mandate handed down to them; they want explanations. Take the time to explain why you make the decisions you make. Better yet, include the teen in the decision-making process.

## IDEALISM

Teens also become extremely idealistic. Another consequence of their developing frontal lobes is the ability to see the world not just as it is but as it could and should be. For the first time, adolescents can imagine a perfect world—and attribute blame for problems they see. This powerful insight expands their perspective but often leads to disenchantment. They wonder how adults could stand by and let global warming, homelessness, and pollution happen. They become critical of the older generation, especially its closest rep-resentatives—their parents. This can be very hurtful if parents take it too personally. A little reminiscing may be the best antidote for parent's hurt feelings. Since time immemorial, after all, each gen-eration has tried to make the world a better place.

## UNCLEAR RULES

One dad decided it was time for his son Matt to mow the lawn, but Matt was already watching television. Dad's exact words were "Matt, the lawn needs to be mowed." Thirty minutes later, Matt was still watching TV. Neuroscientists explain this is not defiance or laziness on the teenager's part, but rather an example of how the teenage brain and the adult brain interpret information differently. To the father, it was perfectly clear that the mowing should commence immediately. His son understood that he was expected to mow the lawn, but did not interpret the intended timeframe as his dad did.

Unclear rules and expectations are a major root of unhappiness between teens and parents. Changes in the adolescent brain predispose teens to misinterpret language. The more specific we can be with our words, the less confusion will result. The parent who says "Don't be late" or "Clean up your room" has left the door open to multiple interpretations. "Late" or "clean" to a teenager may not be the same as late and clean to you. Specific is better. "Be home by 6:00" and "Make your bed and clean up the clothes on the floor" will clarify the expectation.

## CHOOSE YOUR BATTLES

Finding a reason to fight is rarely the problem with teenagers and parents. There is a laundry list of common issues to disagree on. Parents need to sort out which issues are worth fighting about and which are best ignored. Music, eating habits, use of allowance, not doing chores, messy rooms, not wanting to go out with the family, bad attitude, and grammar are all minor episodes in the grand scheme of things. Major issues include things like eating disorders, alcohol and drug abuse, stealing, fighting, promiscuity, and depression. The ability to separate the wheat from the chaff is often lost on the teenager, so a well-thought out parental perspective is essential. A little foreshadowing can diffuse a brewing storm.

Figure 4.1 is a list of common conflicts in the home. Get a head start on parenting by reviewing the items and sorting them into three categories:

1. I need to hold a firm line.
2. I need to negotiate.
3. I need to let it go.

As you peruse this list, remember there is a great deal of difference between the young and old adolescent brains. A young ado-

Social Conflicts
- choice of friends
- choice of dating partners
- how often they can go out
- what kind of activities they can attend
- curfew
- age allowed to date
- riding in cars with friends
- going steady
- clothes and hairstyles

Conflicts about Responsibilities
- chores
- earning and spending money
- keeping rooms neat
- using the car
- using the telephone
- using the computer
- messy bedroom

Conflicts about School
- general attitudes toward classes and teachers
- behavior (disrespectful, tardy, truant)
- homework
- study habits
- grades

Family Conflicts
- showing respect to parents
- quarreling with siblings
- relationship with grandparents

**Figure 4.1. Common Conflicts at Home**

lescent should certainly have an earlier curfew than an older adolescent. Establishing a structure for doing homework may be facilitated by parents for the younger adolescent, but hopefully not for the older teen. Expectations need to be age appropriate to avoid unnecessary disagreements.

## FAST FACTS

- The closer a girl is emotionally to her father, the later she enters puberty.
- The teen brain craves novelty.
- Great athletes emerge during adolescence as the parietal lobes develop.
- Great musicians surface as the parietal lobes develop.
- Emotions help create lifelong memories (good or bad).
- Individuals who use their left and right hands equally have brains with strong connections between the hemispheres; this allows them to remember events, places, and early memories with more ease.

**5**

# SOCIAL LIFE: THE TEEN SCENE

If men are from Mars and women are from Venus, then adolescents are truly from outer space. These bewildering, disturbing, and oh-so-fun extraterrestrials come equipped with a bag full of the weird and wonderful.

## PUTTING THE PUZZLE TOGETHER

Did you know . . .

- . . . adolescents feel pleasure more than adults?
- . . . the corpus callosum houses our feelings of self, and develops during the teen years?
- . . . peer pressure can be a positive force in a teenager's life?
- . . . teenagers are looking for loyalty and commitment? They want to share their deepest and darkest secrets with a friend.

On a scale of 1 to 10 in importance, friends score about 110; they are off the charts for the adolescent. Never is it more important to have something to do on a Friday night, someone to call when you're feeling blue or to instant message when you're feeling good. The following are suggestions for understanding and dealing with specific social issues in your teenagers' life.

## FRIENDS

A twelfth-grade girl, reflecting on friendship and loyalty, remembered this story from eighth grade:

> Becky dumped her boyfriend. He was real popular and he made up all these lies that she had cheated on him and that she was a whore. No one liked her; they kicked her out of our group. This was really hard for me because we were BFF [best friends forever], but I wanted to be in the group. We stayed friends. We were walking down the street towards the Coyote Fair; cars were driving the loop and would yell, "whore" and "slut." She started to cry. I said, 'We don't need to go to the fair." We went home and watched movies. We're still friends today and when they kicked me out of the group she did the same for me.

A teen's interest in peers, which sometimes is all consuming, is also natural. Young children's relationships revolve around the family, but teens stretch beyond the family to form other friendships. The hippocampus, a brain structure responsible for transferring short-term memory into long-term memory, continues to increase in size throughout adolescence and is particularly large in girls. Neuroscientists speculate that this helps girls navigate social situations. (Finally, their brains are developing a skill they value—the ability to party!)

The ability to disclose information properly also comes as the teen matures. They want to share intimate information with a close friend but they need to figure out to whom and what to tell. They eventually learn to realize that not everyone needs to know their deepest and darkest secrets, but they are very liberal with the people they deem confidantes. It can seem at times that close friends never stop talking to each other. They spend the night together, are on the cell phone on the car ride home, and immediately instant message each other upon arrival. This sharing plays an important role in building self-esteem; it helps validate who they are as a person. Finally, they have someone they can trust who understands them and can assure them that their thoughts and feelings are normal. As one girl said, "I feel uncomfortable in that group and my best friend understands why; she feels uncomfortable there, too."

Friendships provide more than someone to talk to; friends instigate, participate, and wallow in fun together. We know teens are attracted to novelty and often their peers supply this in abundance. Get a group of teens together and the good times roll. Teens, like adults and older children, gravitate to those who enjoy similar activities and understand them.

> We all love horses.
> He loves to play computer games and so do I.
> We like the same music and the same TV shows—we like reality
> TV shows and rap and hip-hop—a big mixture.

Loyalty is another element of friendship. Teens are looking for someone they can count on through thick and thin. The importance of understanding and loyalty can be seen in comments such as "One of my friends saw me and said she wanted me to be her friend. She saw that I was insecure and so was she and she wanted to help me" and "They are always there for me if I need them."

*What should parents do?* It's important to foster positive friendships while still offering strong family support. Encourage teens to invite their friends over, make them feel welcome, pop a pizza in the oven, and let the bottled water flow. You may find that you enjoy their company more than you think, and you'll definitely find comfort in knowing that these kids are supervised.

With younger teens, you have greater control over whom they spend time with; after all, you're the one with the car and the wallet. With older teens you have almost no control, but you do have influence. It's important to realize the difference between the two and act accordingly.

Forbidding friendships is very tricky. If a friend represents a real, live threat to your child, the decision is easy, but more often the area is gray and parents should tread lightly. One mother's daughter had questionable parents. After a particularly unsettling incident, she refused to let her daughter sleep over at the friend's house, but she did encourage her to have the girl stay at their home. This wasn't a perfect solution—her daughter was unhappy with her—but it was the mom's attempt to make all parties happy. For what it's worth, her daughter is now an adult and understands the decision; eventually there are happy endings.

Some common activities for teens are:

- Hanging out
- Watching television
- Playing computer games
- Cruising in a car
- Shopping at the mall
- Talking on the phone
- Drinking alcohol

## CONFORMITY

I try to go along with my friends so they won't think I'm weird. Hang out with them at the skate rink, go to movies, and flirt. I just don't want them to think I'm weird.

Adolescence is a period of self-consciousness and self-doubt. Conforming to peers soothes these insecurities. Wearing the right clothes, having the "in" hairstyle, listening to the cool music, and in general looking and thinking like others assures teens that they are okay, that they are in the norm, and that others understand them. They are trying to create the perfect blend of individuality and acceptance.

Teens pick their friends to maximize similarities. Groups and cliques take on their own personalities. One minute everyone in the group is wearing baggy jeans and using the word "phat" to mean "pretty, hot, and thin" and the next they are all in cropped pants with belly button piercings. As Tashina said with excitement, "Sometimes my best friend and I pick out the same outfits, like tomorrow we're wearing camouflage and we wore the same top for picture day."

Conformity is a path to popularity, and the media supplies the map. Brand consciousness seems to increase during the teenage years, and teens feel no hesitation about wearing a designer's name all over their bodies. They rely on brands to project a positive image to others and bolster feelings of self-worth. Teens with low self-esteem are especially attracted to image ads. Maggy, a girl from a lower socioeconomic group, said, "Clothes matter, you just got to look good."

*What should parents do?* As much as possible, support conformity needs of adolescents. Let your kids dress like his or her peers, have similar curfews, and follow the same rules as long as they are reasonable. This is an important part of confirming who they are. Do not make fun of their choices, even when your son appears with burgundy highlights in his hair and a dog collar around his neck. Every generation has its own music, a look that is all its own, and a vocabulary that sets it apart, so don't expect anything less from your teen's generation. Do be aware, however, of the media's message to teens in relation to conformity. It often leads to negative identities and low self-esteem. Chapter 10 goes into technology and the media in greater detail.

## HANGIN' AND TALKIN'

Just hangin' and talkin' is healthy teenage behavior and actually has an important purpose in an adolescent's development. Teenagers learn to make decisions by discussing and mulling over various ideas; brainstorming, reflecting, and rolling things over are all part of the process. This is time-intensive work. Sometimes we watch and wonder as a whole afternoon is spent just discussing what a group of teens are going to do. At the end of the day, they leave for home with the discussion the only part of the activity accomplished. At first glance it seems like a waste of time, but they are actually preparing their brains to take on the adult responsibilities of planning, negotiating, and decision making.

*What should parents do?* Resist the temptation to get involved and suggest activities. Trust me—they do not want our help. A father who kept interjecting opinions was amazed at how none of his helpful ideas were followed or even appreciated. As parents, we need to realize that consensus is an important skill to develop and take into the adult world. What seems like time being wasted is actually time well spent in developing their brain. Leave them alone and let their minds ramble.

## PEER PRESSURE

Peer pressure, as cold as ice. Jackie was confident, seventeen, and knew her own mind. Her town had just received the first ice storm of the season and she and her friends were eager to get out and enjoy the slippery slopes. Their first stop was a nearby lake. Bob, Diane, and John sprinted out onto the lake and luckily found an area that supported their weight. Jackie stood on the edge of the shore, refusing to join them—she knew it wasn't safe. Everyone kept teasing her, "Come on, give me a break! We're all out here, the ice is fine." Finally, feeling the pressure, she ventured out. Within twenty steps of shore she fell through the ice. John, her boyfriend, ran over to rescue her and also fell through. Fortunately, the lake was shallow, they could stand up, but they couldn't climb out; the ice kept breaking. Finally, exhausted and half-frozen, they got out of the water and ran to their truck. Living in the North, they knew enough about hypothermia to strip off their wet clothes. As they returned home, Jackie sat in the truck, naked, embarrassed, with an old, filthy blanket around her. Glancing at her friends, she whispered, "Now I understand peer pressure. I knew it wasn't safe."

Peer pressure—the very phrase sends visions of wild parties, daredevil driving, and sexual experimentation flashing before our eyes. But to teenagers, peers are priceless. They represent fun and acceptance, and they are critical to the development of a teen's identity and self-esteem.

Teens are most influenced by peers during middle adolescence, from about age fourteen to sixteen. It is during these few years that things get out of whack. Peers have the strongest influence over relatively superficial matters such as music preferences, clothing styles, and curfew. Parents are much more influential over religious beliefs, moral values, and political ideas.

Peer pressure is often thought of as a negative, but in reality it is often a positive force in kids' lives. Ninth grade tends to be a pivotal year. The friends teens make, their commitment to school, and the activities they join during this grade sets the tone for their remaining high school years. The right peer group can create a safety net of activities and fun that shields teens from at-risk behavior such as drugs and alcohol, dropping out of school, and promiscuity.

*What should parents do?* Make a point of meeting your teen's friends and open your house to them. Teens who have a lot of unsupervised time are at greater risk for joining gangs, smoking, or drinking. Being welcoming can mean the difference between parenting being easy or difficult.

When engaging your son's or daughter's friends, particularly in the middle school years, play it straight. Teens are particularly sensitive to their friends making judgments about their parents. Do not try to make jokes or do anything that they might construe as embarrassing. Even on your best behavior, you are very likely to mortify your child, but at least you'll have the satisfaction of knowing you did your best. As a rule, when it comes to your kid's friends, the less said, the better.

## DATING, LOVE, AND SEX

"My first boyfriend was in sixth grade. His best friend asked me if I'd go out with him. I said, 'Yes.' I was so excited. The whole time we went out we never talked; one time in the hall, we gave each other a 'high five.' We might still be going out—we never did break up," she said laughing.

Adolescence is an appropriate time to learn about the opposite sex. Estrogen sashays down the school hallways and testosterone thunders toward her. Puberty has ambushed the sexually dormant child. Never will they more easily learn how to get along and do the mating dance than at this time—it is one of those windows of opportunity.

Love is as much a matter of the brain as the heart. During fMRI scans, regions of the brain actually light up when pictures of a girlfriend or boyfriend are shown. Not surprisingly, these parts of the brain are all linked with feeling good. When we feel love, dopamine is released at peak levels into the brain, creating a natural high. Finally, oxytocin streams into the brain, which stirs up feelings of desire and affection. Higher levels in girls' brains encourage nurturing and cuddling, which prepares them for future relationships with children and a significant other. When this biochemical concoction converges on the brain, adolescents are vulnerable to bouts of intense adoration.

The teen brain stays in love for about four months, which is much less time than in adults. This partially explains the short-term relationships often seen in middle and high school. It is only after the brain's rapid change calms down that the frontal lobes can become active and logically reflect on the pros and cons of a relationship. Most adolescents have some romantic relationship between the ages of twelve and eighteen years, although how teens define "love" and "relationship" varies with age. Young adolescents often muse about being in love with a person they don't know well, maybe to whom they have rarely spoken. Older adolescents are more judicious in using the word "love."

Teenagers spend a lot of time picking out the right clothes, practicing what to say, fretting over whether or not feelings are reciprocated. High-schoolers report being consumed a minimum of five hours a week thinking about a real or an imagined relationship; from my own observations, I think this is an underestimation.

A normal activity during dating is some sexual experimentation; kissing and holding hands are both to be expected. Unfortunately, in the United States, more and more teens are engaging in heavy petting and sexual intercourse at younger ages and with multiple partners. Contradicting this trend are the Minnesota Search Institute findings that 42 percent of youths believe that it's important not to be sexually active. Actions and belief systems are obviously not in sync.

*What should parents do?* With all the sexual innuendos (and overt references) on television, in music, and in society in general, you'd think we'd all be very comfortable talking about sex with our kids, but we're not. Even if you feel awkward discussing sex with your teenager, try to break out of your comfort zone. You do have the option of having another person (like an aunt or older brother or sister) broach this topic, but make every effort to overcome your feelings and do it yourself. This openness sends the message that they can count on you when they need guidance.

Three factors play a role in the sexual risk-taking behaviors of adolescents:

1. Parental support
2. Parental control of their behavior
3. Parental psychological control of the teen

It is important to realize that a preoccupation, bordering on obsession, with the opposite sex is normal; be tolerant but vigilant. Monitoring is vital. The sexual tension between teens as they head out on dates is almost tangible, so ensure that adult supervision is in place and more directed activities are arranged as protective shields against irresponsible behavior. Too much free time leads to risky business. At home, talk openly about your expectations; for example, "We expect you to not have sex." Explain your thoughts and be open to their questions.

As nerve-racking as dating can be for parents, teens who don't learn how to get along with the opposite sex often find it hard to have relationships later on. This is truly a combination of normal (for the teen) and stressful (for the parent).

## BREAKUPS

In middle school, breakups are fairly routine and, for the most part, taken in stride. As one girl commented, "I have a boyfriend, not too serious. We've been seeing each other for six months, but I haven't talked to him for two months. I met him at a party and then we talked on the phone and gave each other notes through friends. I think I'll break up with him, but I don't want to hurt his feelings and he seems to be so innocent. It won't take me too long to get over him because I like another guy."

Breakups are much more traumatic in high school. You will see girls weeping in the halls or the star basketball player missing shot after shot after a bad breakup. Breakups are painful at any age, but older teenagers are particularly vulnerable. Their relationship needs are more complex and their coping skills are underdeveloped, so they don't know how to appropriately soothe their pain. Breaking up is one of the most common causes of adolescent depression, suicide, and murder. Additionally, because their identity is not fully formed, a breakup makes teens question who they are in a negative way. The person who initiates the breakup has an easier time of it because he or she already has closure on the relationship, but because the other person was not yet done with the relationship, it is not so easy for him or her to move on. Allow recent recipients of a breakup time to find resolution.

*What should parents do?* Do not underestimate a teenager's pain. Explain that the intense pain is normal; encourage talking it out with you or with their friends. A sympathetic "on call at a moment's notice" listener is one of the best antidotes. It validates their feelings and comforts their feelings of loss. Give permission to slow down and heal. It's common to go through a mini-depression after a breakup; this includes a loss of energy and a desire to sleep.

Suggest that mementos of the relationship be put away (after an appropriate amount of time has elapsed) because they just conjure up unhappy memories. Finally, encourage teens to wait for a while before making any immediate major decisions or changes, too. After one bad breakup a girl, accompanied by a friend, went and got a huge tattoo on her back—not a long-term solution to feeling better!

## TATTOOS, PIERCINGS, AND WHATEVER HAPPENED TO ROCK 'N' ROLL?

Teens constantly try to establish their own identities and autonomy. Unfortunately (or fortunately, depending on your disposition), this often means experimenting with their looks. During my generation, boys wore long hair and were accused of looking like girls. Today the experimenting continues. Usually teens only experiment with something temporary like a hairstyle or hair color, but sometimes it takes a more permanent form with tattoos and piercings. Every generation defines itself by its distinct music; it's almost a rite of passage to shock members of the older generation and garner their disdain.

*What should parents do?* Pick your battles and keep in mind that very likely their desire to do something drastic comes from wanting to fit in with friends or as a point of rebellion—both in the realm of "normal." Next, decide your stance and have a discussion with your teen to see what's on his or her mind. Hopefully you can find a compromise. Perhaps in your family you'll say it's acceptable to dye or spike hair and have a pierced ear, but draw the line at multiple piercings and tattoos. Whatever the final decision, the heart of the issue is the discussion that occurs.

Role modeling of confrontations that are handled through open dialogue is a skill they will take into adulthood. I'm not sure that ending the conversation with the reminder that once they leave home they can do as they please is helpful, but it certainly is frequently used.

One mother asked her daughter every three months what type of tattoo she wanted. Once it was a daisy, another time an ankle vine, and then an Asian symbol on her shoulder. The permanence of the tattoo versus the impermanence of her desires became apparent to her daughter. It was a creative solution that made the point.

If your son and daughter appears at home with the deed done, stay cool. Get more information with responses like "Tell me what's going on," "Oh really?" and, "I'm listening." Keep the lines of communication open first, even if you later decide to impose consequences.

## LONELINESS

For some teenagers, loneliness is a depressing and embarrassing issue. A lonely teen is different from a teen who is comfortable being alone; a lonely teen wants to be with others but feels excluded. Teenagers tend to be lonelier than children and adults. Part of this stems from the fact that teens are culturally conditioned to think they should go out every Friday night and they've been told over and over that these are the best years of their lives. If life isn't bursting with raucous parties and boisterous happenings, they feel deserted, forlorn, and friendless. Teenage boys have more problems with loneliness than girls; this may be because they have difficulty expressing themselves and don't know how to let others know they want to go out.

Lonely teens often lack empathy and have weak social skills. They aren't sure how to relate to others or how to act in different situations. They enter every social situation expecting rejection, and get what they expect. When they are in a group, they tend to talk about themselves instead of asking about the other people. These are the people with whom you can talk to for an hour and leave knowing everything about them, without sharing anything about yourself.

*What should parents do?* Help teens develop healthy coping strategies. Encourage them to join clubs, pick up the phone and call somebody, or take up a new hobby. Nudge them toward taking social risks, call or e-mail someone they would like to get to know. One mother, after listening for weeks how her daughter had no friends, told her daughter that she wanted her to call three people before the weekend. The mother set the expectation, her daughter followed through, and she slowly broadened her group of friends. Being tough was the right tactic at the right time for this teen. It's tricky to know when to nudge the adolescent forward; each has his or her own timeline that needs to be respected.

Alternately, instead of increasing your teen's social network, reduce his or her social expectations. Rather than aiming to go out once a week, let him know it's okay to go out once every two weeks. This goal is easier to meet and therefore it is easier for the teen to feel good about himself.

Independent teens can fill their solitary hours by reading or doing a hobby. Keep a watchful eye out for teens who don't find healthy ways to cope. They are at risk for drowning their troubles in alcohol or drugs.

## FAST FACTS

- Boys and girls are mean in different way, but the effects are equally damaging.
- The average teen begins dating at fifteen.
- Young adolescents usually date in groups.
- Going steady is good for teenagers (security and deeper relationship) and bad for teenagers (greater chance of sexual activity).
- The heart pumps 20 percent of blood to the brain, and the brain uses 20 percent of the oxygen we breathe.
- Neurons in our nose constantly regenerate, but they always remember the information from their predecessor; smell is a powerful memory.
- There is no sense of pain in the brain itself; this allows surgeons to probe while the patient is awake.

**6**

# SURVIVING YOUR
# TEENAGER'S EMOTIONS

**"I** hate you!" "You are such a bitch," and "Screw you"—clear and unsettling evidence that your sweet and innocent child has become a teenager. Emotions run high, patience is at a minimum, and frustration is at a maximum. No wonder even the most confident parent begins questioning his or her parenting skills. Is he or she potentially raising a stable, caring adult or an immature, self-centered monster?

## PUTTING THE PUZZLE TOGETHER

Did you know . . .

- . . . older adolescents can better follow an argument than can younger adolescents?
- . . . teens who are bullies tend to have low self-esteem and conduct disorders?
- . . . abused babies have smaller brains as teenagers?

- . . . teenagers who feel disconnected from their parents are more likely to feel lonely?

A lunch lady at the high school related this story to me about the trials and tribulations of working with teens. She'd had an exhausting day of serving food to over 1,300 students in the span of eighty minutes. The last group to tray-up for lunch were the ninth graders. As she handed the tray to one fifteen-year-old, the girl quickly scanned her tray and noticed that one of her shrimp poppers had made contact with her applesauce. She glared at the lunch lady, and sarcastically said, "That's so gross. If I'm sick the rest of the day, I want you to know it's all your fault." Who can understand this reaction? Not any adults I know, although there is some comfort in knowing that teenagers treat everybody, not just their parents, this way. The following are suggestions in understanding and dealing with your teenager's emotional ups and downs.

## ACTIONS AND CONSEQUENCES

Teenagers try the very souls of adults with some of their actions: not doing homework, smoking cigarettes, hanging with an undesirable crowd. Moms everywhere ask, "Didn't I teach you better than that?" There seems to be a disconnect in the teenage mind between present actions and future consequences.

Neuroscientist Deborah Yurgelun-Todd explains the inner working of the teenage brain: "Good judgment is learned, but you can't learn it if you don't have the necessary hardware." Adolescents don't have the necessary hardware to make good choices. The branching of neurons in the prefrontal cortex becomes much more complex during the teen years. The brain power that is crucial to making good decisions is still in its infancy. Teens simply aren't capable of always realizing the consequences of their actions. Making

them feel bad about it afterwards has about as much effect as trying to teach a two-year-old to drive.

Adolescents are also challenged by the concept of time. It's been
said that a middle-schooler defines the future as 3:00 P.M. (when
school lets out). Such limited vision leads to short-sighted actions.
A better understanding of time kicks in around age fourteen, but
in the meantime it is very difficult for teens to understand possible
future consequences of their actions.

*What should parents do?* The more parents relate actions to immediate consequences, the better the chance that the teen will
make the connection. For instance, a teenager can relate drinking
alcohol to getting kicked off the football team, but will be lost by talk
of jail, treatment centers, and living in halfway houses. They need
consequences they can see and hear now. The abstract, future-
esque consequences of a life in poverty may have meanings for the
adult brain that are lost on the teenage brain.

## ARGUE AND ARGUE

An exasperated mother relayed the following conversation she'd
had with her son: "I began with the simple statement 'You need to
be in by 10:00.' Right out of the shoot, he was angry, 'Why? Nobody else has to be in at 10:00' Calmly, I explained, 'Because it's a
school night.' From there, the conversation deteriorated. He
yelled 'I hate you; I wish I had Corey's parents. They let him stay
out as late as he wants.' After a couple minutes of back and forth
bickering, I lost all composure and said, 'I don't care what Corey's
parents do, I'm your mother and as long as you live in this house
you will follow my rules.' Even in my head it sounded a bit too
much like my own mother. Where did the conversation go wrong?"

Parents can expect an increase in arguments during the teen
years. Boys, cars, computers—sometimes it seems that adolescents

will fight over anything and everything. Changes in the brain increase the likelihood of arguments between teens and parents in two ways. First, the teens' increased mental abilities demand explanations and reasons for decisions that were just accepted as fact during childhood. Second, the emotional part of the brain is in charge, so tears and yelling prevail over calmness. Parents are bewildered by this behavior and wonder how much attitude they should tolerate, what issues are really worth fighting about, and what kind of discipline is effective.

Most homes have about ten minutes of arguing twice a week and are still considered normal. These conflicts tend to arise over everyday matters such as chores and style of dress (minor issues) as opposed to sex and drugs (major issues). In teen girls, menstrual period cycles are associated with increased conflict, especially between mother and daughter. The combination of brain development and estrogen levels leaves the teenage girl swinging back and forth from elation to edgy on a daily basis.

Be forewarned, as teenagers get older, they may be less willing to concede to their parent's wishes. A young teen will reluctantly agree to do homework at your suggestion, while the older teen will consider it an intrusion on his freedom.

Unfortunately, about 20 percent of parents find themselves in constant conflict with their teen. Fights occur frequently and for prolonged periods. A poor parent/teen relationship puts the teen in jeopardy for drug use, dropping out of school, and other at-risk behavior.

*What should parents do?* Don't argue with a teenager. They are not as mentally or emotionally mature as adults and the difference is apparent when it comes to arguing. They are almost always compelled to continue a fight. When an argument arises, calmly and concisely state your views and then stop. Often let them have the last word and walk away. Refer to additional strategies for handling the argumentative teen in "ADHD" and "Anger and Aggression" included in chapter 11.

## CHALLENGING AUTHORITY

Teenagers will challenge almost everything we taught them as children. As much as it hurts, this is actually a good and normal thing. It's important to remember that teens are not personally attacking the parent but instead are finding out who they are as individuals. Questioning and coming to their own conclusions helps create their identity. Instead of blindly believing that they should be a Democrat or a Methodist, teens will challenge those identities and see where they fit into their own lives. Unfortunately, teens often take this to an extreme level and confront parents, teachers, and adults in inappropriate ways. Teens who call adults names and yell inappropriately are crossing the line.

*What should parents do?* Encourage independent thinking. When teens say they want to visit another church, take them. When they argue for an increase in taxes when they know you are dead set against it, listen and let them know when a point makes some sense. As the parent, it is more important to be generous and to let them express themselves than it is to be right.

These actions are usually a mixture of exploring their identity and a mini-rebellion—both are in the norm. The parent who feels threatened and attempts to control these actions and statements is setting the stage for a full-blown rebellion.

Let teens know that overt confrontation, such as cursing or taking swings at people, is not acceptable behavior. Suggest a cooldown period (anywhere from ten minutes to an entire day) during which everyone agrees not to discuss a hot topic until heads have cooled.

## IMPULSE CONTROL (GETTING MAD)

Doug was a good kid, a great kid. He had lots of friends, teachers liked him, and he could be described as a gentle soul. One night after getting off work at the YMCA, he offered a girl he found attractive a ride home on his motorcycle. To his delight, she agreed to the ride. Being the gentleman he was, he gave her the helmet and they started cruising down the road.

What happened next is unexplainable. Did he want to impress her? Was he looking for a little excitement? No one knows for sure. But for a three- or four-block period, Doug full-throttled the bike and they flew down the street. His impulse ended in tragedy. A sixty-seven-year-old woman was crossing the street; she was killed on impact. Doug was thrown fifteen feet onto the cement and died within minutes. The girl did survive, in large part because of the helmet she was wearing, and after months of surgery and physical therapy she recovered. You wish you could attribute this to a freak incident, but unfortunately this scenario is all too common with teenagers.

The connection between the amygdala and the frontal lobes is just beginning to strengthen. In the meantime, the emotional part of the brain is in the driver's seat. It's not a teenager's fault that the brain isn't under control, but it is his or her responsibility to get it under control and it is the parents' responsibility to help. This is a window of opportunity for teenagers. It will never be easier for them to learn to control anger, rage, and frustration. Individuals who do not gain control over their emotions during adolescence turn into the adults who populate anger management classes.

*What should parents do?* Encourage teens to think before they speak or act. Be specific about what is tolerated and what is not: "You cannot call me names" and "Don't hit the wall." The more specific your mandate, the better it will be understood. Do not try to reason with a teen in the middle of an argument. Be patient and save the conversation for when things are cool and calm.

If teens continue to fly out of control, follow through on consequences. Make sure the consequences are logical, fit the crime, and work for both you and the teen. Grounding them for weeks on end is not good for anyone; besides, it soon loses its effectiveness.

As you contemplate a proper consequence, remember that communication, as discussed in chapter 3, is the most effective way to change teenage behavior.

If you feel you are the one out of control and have thrown out a consequence that no one could or should have to live with, give yourself time to calm down and then explain to the teen that you overreacted and are reducing the punishment. This will not be seen as a sign of weakness, but instead as a sign of reconciliation.

## INDESTRUCTIBLE AND IMMORTAL

Because of the changes occurring in their brains, teenagers feel that nothing bad can happen to them. This blindness explains the risky behavior they actively pursue, such as unprotected sex (she won't be the one to get pregnant), driving recklessly (he won't be injured or killed), or swimming in a river (they won't be swept away).

*What should parents do?* Our best defense against this type of behavior is monitoring and doing our best to curb risky activities. Talk to them about unprotected sex and STDs; our country has the highest number of STDs of any industrialized nation and experts believe it is because we encourage ignorance about STDs. Open the door to conversation—but back it up with supervision.

Require them to wear helmets when they skateboard or bike to protect the brain. It you think something isn't prudent, don't let them do it. A father's youngest son wanted to drive to a basketball game in a nearby town on a foggy night when visibility was very limited. Many of his friends were going despite the precarious weather. The father told his son he couldn't go to the game, but then showed him respect by explaining why. His son wasn't happy about it, but he accepted the decision.

My community faced an unprecedented number of adolescent drinking and driving deaths last year. Schools began to show graphic movies of what can happen under these circumstances. In the short run, shocking images curtail risky behavior; combine those images with parental monitoring to best protect teens from themselves.

## MALE AGGRESSION

Misreading information is not the only reason that emotions reign supreme in teenagers. Aggression, anger, and sexual interest all contribute, and puberty escalates the situation. Once puberty strikes, boys receive approximately 1,000 times more testosterone than they did as children, about ten jolts a day. This overstimulates the amygdala (which is already enlarged in the adolescent boy), which is also associated with aggression and sexual interest. A potentially logical discussion about whose turn it is to mow the lawn can easily explode into an argument. When confronted, boys are perfectly primed to say things like "Why should I have to? Billy doesn't have to!"

*What should parents do?* Now is the time to help boys learn impulse control; refer to suggestions described above in "Impulse Control (Getting Mad)." In addition, set reasonable expectations for them; for example, they can go into their room and yell, but they cannot scream at you. Teach coping skills, such as exercise; identify trigger words such as "Because I said so" or "I'm disgusted with you"; and then teach age-appropriate ways to handle them. Praise the proper handling of issues; everyone needs to hear a good word every now and then—be generous.

## RECKLESS BEHAVIOR

Eighty percent of teens report engaging in one or more risky behaviors during a month. They commit transgressions such as disobeying parents, school misconduct, substance abuse, driving while intoxicated, having unprotected sex, theft, or fighting. Why are they doing this? Adolescents experience more intense urges than children and adults, and the mental controls to stop themselves are in short supply. The abilities to plan, monitor, evaluate, and reflect are lacking, so reckless behavior becomes the norm rather than the exception. Increased dopamine levels (feeing good) and decreased serotonin (the calming agent) just add to their desire for novel, risky, and intense stimuli. One study of teen drivers showed that if they were driving alone or with parents, they stopped at a yellow light, an indication of safe driving. But if a peer was riding shotgun, they ran the yellow light. Teens thought this risky behavior had a positive social impact (my friend thinks I'm cool) and found that it was emotionally arousing (this is exciting).

*What should parents do?* When young children have the impulse to do something reckless, they almost always have an adult brain to keep them in check. In contrast, adolescents are seeking autonomy and independence so they make an effort to push that adult brain away. Teens need supervision—surrogate frontal lobes—to effectively support their brain development.

First, adjust your expectations and realize teens will take risks. Next, monitor and prohibit risky and dangerous behavior. Set clear limits and enforce consequences fairly (counting to ten or twenty before addressing a problem may help you stay fair).

Encourage extracurricular activities. Keep them active in positive programs that are meaningful to them. Support middle-school after-school programs in your community, because supervision translates into safety. In my community, young juvenile crime decreased by 42 percent the first year our middle-school after-school programs started. The local police force attributed the reduction to the after-school program.

Most important, bond with your child. Creating a spirit of belonging in the family acts as a protective factor. Let teens know that you are interested in them and their safety. Reassure them that you are with them through thick and thin. More information on reckless behavior and the at-risk teen can be found in chapter 11.

## MOOD SWINGS

Mood swings are common in girls during the teenage years. Chemicals in the brain—norepinephrine and epinephrine (energizers), serotonin (calming), and dopamine (feel good)—percolate in everyone, but during puberty high levels of estrogen contribute to girls' mood swings. One moment everything is wonderful in their world, and the next minute (and I do mean minute—girls moods can change very quickly during adolescence) they think they are ugly, have no friends, and are convinced that no one cares about or understands them.

*What should parents do?* Showing a bit of understanding and tolerance sets the stage for a more tranquil and peaceful adjustment. But again, you do not have to let mood swings be excuses for abusing you. Remind girls of appropriate behaviors.

## HYPOCRISY

"Adolescent hypocrisy" sounds worse than it is and is a normal part of growing up. An adult who is called a hypocrite has just been hit with a direct, unmitigated insult. This same term when referring to an adolescent does not refer to a character flaw, but rather a part of the brain's development. The younger adolescent will often talk or even preach about a strong conviction they hold and then totally ignore it in their actions. For instance, adolescents will talk about truth being important and then lie to their parents, or criticize their parents for not recycling and then throw a candy wrapper on the ground.

*What should parents do?* Ignore and tolerate these situations. A reprimand or suggestion to pick up the wrappers is a good idea. A lecture on how they are saying one thing and doing another is probably meaningless until the hardware in their brains catches up with their good intentions.

This attribute diminishes by high school, when we see kids be-coming actively involved in their communities. Older adolescents not only talk the talk, they walk the walk too. Build on this new ca-pability by encouraging active involvement in service projects.

## NO ONE HAS EVER FELT THE WAY I DO

Brain changes often make teens believe they are the first and only ones to experience anything. Whether it's a breakup, forgetting their locker combination, or cheering a winning team, no one else has ever experienced it. No wonder they think their parents do not understand them! After all, how could they when their parents have never felt like they do?

One mother was trying to comfort her heartbroken daughter af-ter a painful breakup, when the girl looked at her through tear-stained eyes and moaned, "How would you know how I feel? You've never been in love." Rather than countering with the logi-cal and obvious, "What about Dad?" Mom chose to show compas-sion and held her tongue.

*What should parents do?* It would be wonderful if there were some magical solution to curb this feeling, but as parents our best bet is to be aware and then be tolerant. This too will pass.

## STRESS

Small and moderate amounts of stress are good. Without stress, we would fall asleep in class and daydream while driving. When an in-dividual is moderately stressed, adrenaline is released into the body and the body becomes alert, ready to adjust and react to sit-uations. It directs our attention and enhances our memory.

However, adolescents have a great vulnerability to environmen-tal toxins and stresses. If stress persists, the steroid hormone cortisol is released. Cortisol takes a long time to leave the body. It causes the immune system to fall apart (which is why we get sick when we're under a great deal of stress), triggers an increase in heart rates and blood pressure, and makes remembering things difficult. When you are in the stress of a verbal fight, it's hard to think of a perfect comeback; during important exams, answers to test questions pop into your head only *after* you've left the classroom.

Once stressed, teens require a more lengthy recovery time than adults. Teenage girls are particularly at risk. Progesterone, which is released in larger amounts with puberty, lets cortisol run rampant. Once a teenage girl becomes stressed, it is very difficult to get her physically and mentally under control.

*What should parents do?* Talk about the stress you felt when you were a teenager. Often parents are very hesitant to show their human and vulnerable side to their kids. The parent who discloses some information about his own adolescence may hear a huge sigh of relief from his teenager. One father mentioned to his son how he had been so intimidated by girls during high school that he crossed the street so that he wouldn't have to run into them. A look of astonishment appeared on his son's face; he had never considered that his father might have felt this type of self-doubt and intimidation, and took comfort in realizing that his dad had similar worries and insecurities. Dad turned out okay—maybe he would too.

It is important to use discretion with what you share; it's not prudent to go into a dark period of your past. For instance, one parent told his kids how he used to smoke pot, tried cocaine, got arrested, and ended the liturgy with "but I turned out fine." His intentions may have been good, but he is really not reducing teenage stress or being a good role model.

The following is a list of ways to help teenagers reduce stress levels:

- Encourage physical exercise and sports. They release chemicals that make us feel happy and reduce stress.

- Don't burden teenagers with your personal adult problems.
- Talk with teens about their worries.
- Compliment them.
- Use humor.
- Don't overload their schedule.
- Be a role model of self-control and appropriate coping skills.
- Don't expect perfection. Assure teens with comments like "Giving it a try is what is important."
- Encourage relationships outside the family.
- Use competition carefully.
- Suggest meditation and deep breathing.
- Explain that drugs and alcohol increase stress and reduce healthy coping skills.
- Seek professional help if you believe stress is a serious problem.

## FAST FACTS

- Love and pleasure reduce the emotions of anger and stress.
- A fully functioning emotional brain is important in decision making.
- Emotions travel faster to the brain than any other type of information.
- The emotional part of the brain does not reach maturation until the person is about twenty years old.
- People with high emotional intelligence are more supportive of others.
- Overactivity in the emotional brain is linked to teenagers with emotional and/or behavioral disorders.

**7**

# PHYSICAL CHANGES: UNDER CONSTRUCTION

Estrogen, androgen, testosterone—the hormones are free, free at last—and with them comes an array of unusual questions. What is that smell? Why aren't you wearing a bra? Who said you could nap during breakfast? As you sink your teeth into this chapter, keep in mind that the physical changes your teenager is experiencing are normal, individual, and perplexing.

## PUTTING THE PUZZLE TOGETHER

Did you know . . .

- . . . boys and girls really do have different brains?
- . . . sleep patterns change during adolescence?
- . . . exercise stimulates new cell growth in the brain? Exercise can increase mental abilities 20 to 30 percent.
- . . . puberty starts in the brain, not with hormones?

The teenage body is changing from that of a child to an adult. As a parent, you know the importance of eating right, getting plenty of sleep, and developing a positive physical self-image. And yet your son or daughter, the fruit of your loins, is constantly swigging soda pop and munching on nachos, up until all hours of the night, and seems incredibly uncomfortable with the way his or her body is morphing. This is not going to be an easy transition for anyone, individually or as a family unit. The following are different issues that come into play for the teenager as they change from an asexual child to a sexual adult.

## PUBERTY

Storm and stress.
   I hated everything that changed: getting taller, getting breasts, getting acne. . . . It was all different—change, change, change.
   Worrying that someone was going to call and ask me to go swimming and I wasn't sure how to use a tampon.
   What do you mean, you're wearing your Dad's shoes?

Puberty starts when the hypothalamus sets it into motion— around age eleven for girls and thirteen for boys. Estrogen and testosterone wash over the brain and everything begins to change in seemingly random ways: whiskers, breasts, menstrual periods, wet dreams, and getting taller and lankier by the minute. The rapid growth and wide variation between individuals make teens hypersensitive to their appearance. There are late bloomers and early bloomers, and nobody feels like a just-right bloomer. At no other time is self-esteem so closely connected to body image. Normally, body image influences only about 25 percent of self-esteem, but during the teen years it can dominate.

*What should parents do?* As parents, our goal is to help adolescents adjust to their new bodies. Talk to your teen about what's happening physically. Research shows that boys and girls who are knowledgeable about puberty have an easier transition through it. Never tease a kid about physical looks. One girl experimented with hair dye and found herself looking a bit like Lucy Ricardo from the *I Love Lucy* show. Instead of trying to make the best of it, her father made jokes about her looking like a clown. Another mom always pointed out her son's acne to her friends as though he weren't in the room. These blatant examples of insensitivity cut deep into the adolescent's heart. In my opinion, neither parent fully understood the damage his or her words were doing.

The next thing we can do to help teens adjust to puberty is to take their focus off their bodies. Compliment them on something besides their looks. It's amazing how many compliments are given strictly on a person's hair, face, or clothing. Spotlighting something besides looks is healthy for all teens. This is a particularly important strategy for teens with eating disorders where body image consumes their thoughts.

Keep them engaged in things they liked as children. If they liked sports, encourage them to stay in sports; if they liked singing, encourage that. Often girls lose their childhood interests and become overly interested in what the media tells them is important (such as becoming sexual objects). Participation in activities can be an antidote to the media's message. And don't jump to conclusions about what is going through their heads. Being interested in sex and their bodies is normal and should not be interpreted as being sexually active.

Because teens are beginning to move outside the family, this is a perfect time to get them involved in the community and nonprofit organizations. Volunteering is a powerful tool for taking the focus off of themselves and reestablishing it on people who can benefit from their help. Volunteers do meaningful work that reinforces the adolescent positive self-image and forms multigenerational relationships that help reinforce a healthy perspective of life. Community service can run the gamut from enlisting in a highly structured national organization, like a blood bank, or simply visiting nursing homes regularly.

## GAYS AND LESBIANS

All my girlfriends make out at parties. Only one is really gay, I figure I'm about one-third gay. I'm not out to my family. My family is very homophobic, passive in theory, but reality is, it would be an issue. All my friends are okay with it. Our generation is much more accepting of experimentation.

Brain differences have been found between gay and straight males. The hypothalamus, a part of the brain in charge of pain, pleasure, thirst, hunger, and sexual drive, is found to be smaller and thinner in gay males. It is similar in size to heterosexual females (as opposed to the larger and thicker hypothalamus found in heterosexual males). To date, no brain differences have been found with lesbians, although the gay female body has its own physical differences. For example, their inner ear is configured differently from the straight female ear and their fingerprints have a differing number of points.

*What should parents do?* If your child comes out to you, realize that he or she has probably spent many hours preparing for this conversation and that he or she is probably very nervous. Growing up in a community that may not approve of gay lifestyles makes it impossible for them to predict how this news will be received. Remember that your son or daughter has not changed; he or she is the same person that you've been having dinner with and taking to school for years. Be honest about your feelings and deal with feelings first, yours and your teen's. More important, be a good listener and let your teen speak. That being said, if you do find yourself too shocked or too negative to have a conversation, tell your teenager that you need time to digest this news and set a time for further discussion. It's better to delay the talk than say something you will later regret.

Common questions to ask are:

- How long have you know you are gay?
- Has it been hard to carry this secret?
- What can I do to help?

Denying homosexuality and being unsupportive are contributing factors in the cases of half of all runaways, one-third of suicides, and alcohol and drug abuse. If your teen needs additional support, help him or her connect with a support group or counselor.

## EATING HABITS

Eating habits are usually established during the childhood years, strayed from during adolescence, and returned to during adulthood. In the normal-weight teen, nutrients first go to vital organs such as the heart and kidneys, then to skeletal and muscle growth, and finally to thinking in the brain. About half of teens eat five times a day, which can actually be a healthy routine if nutritious foods are eaten (blueberries, beans, broccoli, oats, oranges, pumpkin, salmon, soy, spinach, tea, tomatoes, turkey, walnuts, and yogurt are all considered healthy brain food).

Eating has become much more of an issue during the past decade with unrealistic media expectations of body shape and a rise in eating disorders such as obesity, anorexia, and bulimia. Eating disorders generally originate in the adolescent years.

The brain plays a role in eating disorders. Obesity has been linked to leptin in the brain, a neurotransmitter that notifies the brain that the stomach is full. Teenagers who are obese are probably not properly receiving the leptin message. Without this message, they continue to eat more and more. There also tend to be fewer dopamine receptors in an obese person's brain. Because dopamine is released after a satisfying meal, a plate of chicken Alfredo or chocolate cake leaves us with a feeling of satisfaction. This feeling does not register with obese people until they have gorged themselves, which leads to further weight gain. All of this is compounded by our environment. The availability of fast food and larger portions, and an increase in sedentary activities such as watching television and playing on the computer, only compounds the problem.

Eating disorders may seem like the norm to teenagers. As one girl put it, "My friends would go through stages. They would puke for three days, then get hungry, gain weight, and it would start all over. They were constantly saying, 'Oh my God, I'm so fat.' or 'Oh, I've lost three pounds.' I know there were other girls in school that had serious problems."

Though anorexia and bulimia have primarily cultural origins, the brain does play a small role in these disorders. Some sufferers of anorexia and bulimia have elevated amounts of serotonin, a chemical in the brain that helps regulate moods and behaviors. The compulsion they feel about food (to eat or not eat) is aggravated by increased serotonin levels that tend to increase compulsive behavior. Over an extended period of time, anorexia and bulimia cause a loss of brain matter, putting in jeopardy the quality of all decisions they make, including those concerning food.

*What should parents do?* Parents can help by providing healthy snacks and meals at home. This ensures most teens eat a healthy breakfast and dinner (and two meals out of three is not bad). Accept some changes in their eating behaviors. Don't be surprised to find teens rummaging through the refrigerator at all hours. And get your pocketbook ready—during growth spurts, teens can literally eat you out of house and home.

Suggestions for combating eating disorders:

- Model good eating habits.
- Eat as a family.
- Don't constantly talk about weight or emphasize diets.
- Encourage interests and activities. Hobbies and skills enhance self-esteem, a protective factor.
- Talk about magazine photos and the techniques (like airbrushing) used to achieve unrealistic representations.
- Get professional help when required—recovery is possible.

## SLEEP

Remember the six-year-old who couldn't wait to wake up at 7:00 A.M., eat a bowl of cereal, and watch cartoons? Now she's the sixteen-year-old who wants to sleep until noon and has to be dragged out of bed each morning. What happened? First of all, adolescents need approximately one more hour of sleep each night than adults do. Second, melatonin, nature's sleeping pill, is released at a different time in the brain of teenagers. This results in teens sleeping later in the morning and drifting off to sleep later at night.

The amount of sleep we get affects the way we think, act, and look. Parents, with the best of intentions, may insist that a teenager hit the sack at an appropriate time according to the adult clock, but they should not be surprised to learn that their teen spends the time wide awake staring at the ceiling. Adolescents cannot fall asleep just because their parents said so.

Parents can cater to teen sleeping patterns on the weekends, but the real world does not revolve around them. Unfortunately, about 20 percent of teens are severely sleep deprived. The consequences of sleep deprivation are harsh. Exhaustion results in more difficulty focusing and learning at school, and overemotional reactions to stressors. The sleep-deprived teen will burst into tears or become argumentative with little provocation. Sleep deprivation also leads to difficulty processing glucose, which results in excessive weight gain and obesity.

*What should parents do?* Calming activities right before bed set the stage for snoozing. Get teens in the habit of reading a book, listening to music, or journaling. These types of activities help them relax mentally and physically. Nighttime is not the time to exercise, watch a thriller movie, or get into an argument. Arguing about bedtime at bedtime (a too-common occurrence) simply exacerbates the problem.

Parents can mandate a bedtime for younger adolescents. If that doesn't work, discussing and negotiating a bedtime usually does.

One effective strategy is to let an older teen stay up too late on a school night and then suffer the consequences the next day. This technique often creates an incentive to modify sleep patterns with no nagging from you—especially if you leave "I told you so" out of the conversation. Older adolescents, by and large, should be left alone when it comes to deciding when they should hit the sack.

If you believe your teen is sleep deprived, make gradual changes in his or her sleep patterns, perhaps as gradual as ten minutes a week. Small increments have been shown to be effective in changing sleep schedules. Keeping the room as dark as possible with heavy shades and eliminating the nightlight (unless your teen really does need one) aid in sound sleeping.

Informed and proactive schools are setting later start times for middle and high school students, but the majority of schools still start the day to suit an adult timetable. If you're politically inclined, start a discussion about this with your local school board. The research will support you. Not only would teens do better in school with a later start, but the majority of juvenile crime and teenage pregnancy incidents occur between 3:00 and 6:00 P.M. (when parents are working and kids are unsupervised). School hours that extend later into the afternoon would shield them from risky temptations.

Binge sleeping on the weekends does not solve long-term sleep problems, but do let them sleep in. They will love you for it.

## FAST FACTS (FOR SLEEP)

- Dolphins never close their eyes and completely fall asleep. One side of the brain sleeps first, and then the other.
- Teens require more sleep than preteens or adults.
- Seventy percent of teens have difficulty waking up in the morning.
- Sixty-four percent of teens feel tired during class.

- Drowsiness accounts for more than half of car crashes in drivers age twenty-five and younger.
- On average, teens are getting about seven and a half hours of sleep a night, but need nine and a quarter hours.
- Performance in classes that occur during the first and second periods of school is reduced, indicating that teens suffer from sleep deprivation.

**8**

# GETTING AN EDUCATION

Teenagers spend the bulk of their waking hours at school, learning algebra, literature, and science. Interacting with teachers, peers, lunch ladies, and secretaries, they learn how to navigate the social scene as well as the academic one. Appropriate parental involvement at the middle and high school levels influences the teenager and acts as a shield against dropping out, pregnancy, and drug use.

## PUTTING THE PUZZLE TOGETHER

Did you know . . .

- . . . teenagers are unable to make complex judgments until their mid-twenties?
- . . . teenagers solve problems with greater understanding and better results when they work with other teenagers, although it often takes longer to come to a conclusion?
- . . . teenage language skills are continually improving? They understand symbolism and irony.

- . . . a teenager's belief in his or her ability is a powerful motivating force in school?

The seventh-grader came home from school blazing mad, slammed his books on the counter, and began to regale how his teacher had yelled at him in front of the entire class. His mother was immediately upset, angry, and ready to throttle the teacher, but she also knew her son and so she calmly asked, "What did she yell?" Wherein her son replied, "She yelled, 'Jeffrey Atkinson, get out of my chair!'" The mother logically responded, "Why were you in her chair?' And her son said, "Mrs. Kiley left the room to talk to another student and so I thought I'd take over." Oh dear, unacceptable school behavior! This chapter tackles actual issues that parents deal with with their resident scholar.

## EXPLORE A VARIETY OF SUBJECTS AND ACTIVITIES

Teenagers are drawn to novelty like a moth to a flame. Children, adult, and elderly brains are also drawn to the new and different but, during adolescence, the attractions of novelty rise to a whole new level. When teens do something out of the ordinary, dopamine surges and streams throughout the brain, leaving them giddy with desire and wanting more. This partially explains their infatuation with technology, the latest music, and new power drinks—all drip with novelty and constantly change and modify.

In a curious way, this hunt for novelty has an impact on identity formation. An individual's identity development has two influences: exploration of roles (student, athlete, musician) and attributes of significant people in their lives (compassion in mom, extrovert in dad). Exploring new hobbies and interests is a normal part of the teen experience. Some of this will be the weird and wacky (painting their bodies orange and black for the homecoming game), but other experiments will be more traditional and socially accepted (learning to cook).

*What should parents do?* Encourage teenagers to try new and different things. They need to be free to experiment and then change course if it's not their path. Decisions don't have to be lifetime commitments at this age. One young teenager, Rachel, took violin for one year in fourth grade. As an eleventh grader, she decided to give it another try, but it still didn't stick. Around this same time, however, she decided to try dance. Now, she loves to salsa and merengue.

Help adolescents realize their own dreams. If they are interested in art, register them in art classes; if they like science, enroll them in a summer science institute; if their passion is football, sign them up for football camps.

Don't try to live your life through them. You may have always wanted to be the professional athlete or cheerleader, but it's unfair for them to carry the burden of fulfilling your ambitions. You had your chance, now it's their turn. This attitude is particularly disastrous for a teen who doesn't have the aptitude or interest in the parents' goals. Perhaps Dad was a great pitcher, scouted by the pros, but his son has trouble getting the ball across the plate—ouch!

Encourage other adults to spend time with your teen too. Relatives and neighbors can play an important role expanding awareness of opportunities and activities that they may not know exist.

## HOMEWORK: FORGETFULNESS
## AND DISORGANIZATION

One middle-schooler after another forgets his or her homework. One girl left her pants at a friend's house and didn't remember to get them for three weeks. These absent-minded teens are the norm, not the exceptions.

Forgetful, disorganized, and late for everything but dinner— teenagers can seem like whirling dervishes. This flakiness is related to the changes going on in their brain. Remembering and organizing require a temporary mental workspace—a working memory—which is still developing throughout adolescence. Furthermore, all of the development and new capabilities of the brain make it difficult for reminders to stick. Teen can literally forget immediately what you or their teacher just said. Middle school kids forget their books at school when there's homework and forget to take their books to school from home. And just when you're ready to give up, they turn and inform you that, "It's all your fault!"

The most frustrating can be the homework that is never turned in and the subsequent explanation something like "It was only worth five points." This brings up issues of responsibility and dependability, not to mention an easy way to raise the teen's grade.

I think that the eighth and ninth grades were the most frustrating with my children. I expected more from them (after all, they were almost in high school) but instead I was constantly picking up the slack. I found myself running to the fabric store the night before Consumer Science class so my daughter could make a pair of drawstring shorts, and begging the custodian to let us in the building to retrieve a history book for tomorrow's test. It was encouraging to see great improvement in the tenth grade. I learned it was just a matter of surviving until then.

*What should parents do?* When adolescents do forget something, don't say, "I told you so"—their brains really are not prepared to be perfect. Be forewarned you'll need to find the balance between picking up the slack and letting them suffer the consequences. There will be times when you will run the forgotten homework to school (everybody forgets something sometimes) and other times when they will just have to do without.

When they do remember something important, praise them. It's amazing how often praise and kind words are overlooked during adolescence. Simple comments like "It looks like you worked hard on that paper" or "You really seem to understand math" are music to their ears. If need be, consciously decide that you are going to say one or two positive things to your teen each day.

Reminders are important, so help them keep a calendar and use a school planner—great life skills. School administrators can help here. A principal at one middle school randomly went to one room each week, checked three students' planners, and threw a class pizza party if they were up to date. This was a strong incentive to start a good habit.

## MAKING SIMPLE ASSIGNMENTS COMPLEX

Making simple tasks complex is a preoccupation of young adolescents. Middle school teachers see it on a daily, if not hourly, basis. The young adolescent is given a relatively simple homework assignment and, before you know it, he or she has blown it all out of proportion. Instead of having to do a simple math equation, they rework it as a problem that would bring Einstein to his knees. Their awkward analyses of problems and situations lie in the modifications going on in their frontal lobes. It is good that abstract thinking is developing, but the young adolescent isn't very good at managing it. The result is inept attempts to apply abstract thought.

Teenagers also make the simple into the complex as they navigate social situations. Everyone knows that the simplest approach—being yourself—is the best way to make friends. Young adolescents opt for a more complicated solution. They will go to extremes to make friends, trying to impress others by being too loud or too strange, often generating the opposite response from what they were seeking.

*What should parents do?* Be patient. Stay calm, because they won't. And when it comes to homework, the later the hour, the more emotional the scene will be. If it's school related, a quick call to the teacher for clarification may solve the problem and get everyone on the same page.

Be hands-on. Continue to give them practice solving complex problems, such as "What should our family/community do about creating a green environment?" or "What do you think about immigration into the United States?" Encourage enrolling in challenging, but not frustrating, classes in school; grow a better brain by active involvement in math, language arts, science, and foreign language.

## TRANSITIONING TO MIDDLE SCHOOL OR HIGH SCHOOL

The transitions between middle and high school can be threatening and scary. This is a major life event for adolescents, and in many ways their brains are ill-equipped to handle it. The new school is often more demanding, with higher academic and behavioral expectations. Teens may find themselves without any close friends in class or even (more important) during lunch. Middle school can seem even more threatening than high school. By high school, at least they have already made a major school transition (they know they can do it) and are more mature. It is not uncommon to see students before middle school totally stressed out.

*What should parents do?* Often schools offer opportunities for families to visit ahead of time. Take advantage of this, get your teen's class schedule, and then do a couple of dry runs. If the school doesn't offer a scheduled previsit, call and arrange one. Dreams of being unable to remember locker combinations still haunt adults. Take your teen to school and let him practice opening his locker over and over again. Familiarity breeds comfort.

If adolescents want to talk about their worries, listen and take their concerns seriously. Very likely, their major fears will concern who is in their classes, their teacher ("Please don't let me get the homework queen!"), and if there is a friend in their lunch period. These are deal breakers for the young teen, and your ability to listen and nod can make the difference between an easy or difficult adjustment. Anxiety tends to dramatically decrease after the first month or even week of the school year.

## FAST FACTS

- Left- or right-handedness appears before birth; whichever thumb the baby sucks in the womb will be his or her hand preference.
- Deception is most easily detected in the right hemisphere, so listening with your left ear is most effective.
- Using gestures when you talk engages the right hemisphere of the brain.
- Exercise prevents the brain's dopamine neurons from withering.
- Complex math problems really do require more brain power! They involve more areas of the brain.
- Students with close bonds to their parents are less likely to drop out of school.
- Children who are born prematurely are at high risk for dropping out of school as teenagers.

**9**

# THE FAMILY RULES

"**R**ules were made to be broken." I don't think there is a question in anyone's mind that this phrase was first uttered by a teenager. Curfew, driving, and dating are all fair game when it comes to making and breaking the rules. Creating a happy, supportive home is the goal of all parents, and with a little adult guidance it can become a reality.

## PUTTING THE PUZZLE TOGETHER

Did you know . . .

- . . . older adolescents are more deliberate and systematic problem solvers than younger adolescents?
- . . . new drivers are slow to recognize potential dangers while driving?
- . . . young drivers overestimate their ability to deal with problems on the road?
- . . . as the teenage brain develops, the teen tends to agree more with his or her parents and argues less?

A family was struggling with the normal challenges of raising two teenagers. By all accounts, the two were good boys, but like all teenagers they had their moments. In an effort to strengthen their parenting skills, Mom and Dad decided to join a parenting group and then quickly purchased the moderator's recommended book. Months later, neither had opened the book and pretty much had forgotten its existence. So you can only imagine Dad's surprise when he came upon his son reading that very parenting book in the laundry room. As Dad approached his son, who for all practical purposes had almost finished the book, the boy looked up at him and said, "Boy, you and Mom are really doing a lot of things wrong." Needless to say, these were not the words Dad was hoping for. Beauty (and truth) is in the eye of the beholder. This chapter covers particular issues that every family faces.


## CURFEW

You can't help it. You find yourself pacing the room, watching the clock, feeling a mix of anger and worry thirty minutes after your teen's 11 P.M. curfew. Thoughts of injuries and accidents creep into your mind along with thoughts of how irresponsible your child is and what you will do as soon as she comes home! When she does come home, your "Where have you been?" is met, not with an apology or remorse, but with an accusation—"Why can't I stay out later? Everybody else does! It's not fair! You don't get me."

Setting and meeting curfews are prime battlegrounds for teen and parental confrontations. Because teens tend to operate on the pleasure principle, they do whatever sounds fun. Staying out late and hanging longer with friends are temptations that are difficult to resist.

*What should parents do?* Be proactive. Negotiate with your teenager a fair curfew before missing curfew becomes a problem. Set a curfew that you believe reflects their age and maturity. A teenager who is rarely in trouble and tends to make good choices should have a later curfew than the teen who is constantly in trouble. Be flexible; if there is a special event that merits a later curfew, accommodate this.

It may help to go so far as to draw up a contract that includes concessions by both parties. The contract comes in handy for deescalating the tension if or when they do come in late. Because everyone agreed in advance—under neutral circumstances—that the established curfew was fair, there are no grounds for argument. Also agree on a routine to use in case something legitimate and unforeseen comes up that will make your teenager late, like a phone call about the situation well in advance of the curfew's deadline.

Not arguing does not mean ignoring late returns. When a teenager walks in the door after the established time, address it with a reminder, such as "You know you were supposed to be home by 11:00. Now, it's 11:15. Next time, be on time." This statement clarifies your curfew expectation, which keeps your teen accountable for remembering. If this same scene is repeated on a weekly basis, you may choose to invoke a punishment. If a teen continually comes in very late without calling, consequences are definitely in order.

## DRIVING

Nothing creates more teenage excitement or parental angst than the car. The freedom that a car brings is tempered by the responsibility it requires. Granted, teenagers have many advantages as drivers—their reflexes are in tip-top shape and their vision will never be better—but the prefrontal cortex is still developing. Risk taking ("I can beat the red light"), multitasking ("I always talk on my cell phone and sip soda while I drive"), and making poor decisions ("I only had one beer") are all limitations to the teenage brain's ability to drive safely.

*What should parents do?* Parents need to be models of good driving themselves—no speeding or tailgating, and seatbelts are always buckled. One driver education teacher was a particularly good role model, and he commented on the other drivers he encountered. He'd say things like "I guess Aunt Josie [he always gave them a name] is in a rush today, so I better let her into my lane" and "George seems to be riding pretty close; maybe I should let him pass." These were memorable lessons in how to control emotions while driving, and eliminate potential risks and hazards from other vehicles.

Enroll teens in drivers' education classes and have them drive with you for about six months before turning them loose on the road; gradually loosen the restrictions. At first, only allow them to drive to school and other places you designate. For at least one month, insist that they turn off the radio, CDs, or any other distracters, so their entire focus can be on driving. Don't allow them to drive with friends for the first six months; friends are the king of distractions. Don't allow other teens to drive your car, this is not being mean, this is being smart. Finally, remind teens that use of the car is a privilege, not a right. If they are in an accident or they receive a ticket, they should pay all reasonable financial costs or work in kind. Loss of car privileges or other consequences should be determined on an individual basis.

Some rules of the road:

- Require drivers' education.
- Drive with an adult for the first six months (or about 1,000 miles).
- Drive without distractions for up to six months (eliminate music and friends).
- Ban the use of cell phones while driving (and set a good example).
- Be a good role model by being a safe and courteous driver.
- Slowly increase the circumstances in which teens are allowed to drive.

## TEENAGERS EMBARRASSED
## TO BE SEEN WITH FAMILY

When my dad picks me up from school, he waits on the other side of the street. I just stay on this side and talk to my friends until my little brother gets out, then I go over so we can leave right away.

My mom ran out on the football field when I got hit and she was yelling at everybody—really embarrassing.

Teenagers are very self-conscious. Their brains are beginning to develop a sense of self and they often interpret their own intense interest in themselves as an intense interest by everyone else. One result of this self-consciousness is that they believe they are always on stage with a critical audience watching their every move. If they misspeak, everyone hears it; if they misstep, everyone sees it.

Adolescent self-consciousness is coupled with their newfound capability to envision. Young children can't envision very well, and parents profit from this inability. We are forever protected in the young child's brain because few of our flaws are apparent to him or her. But when dendrites sprout within the adolescent brain, suddenly parents don't know how to dress, walk, or talk. The reason for this lies in the brain. The teen can now construct an ideal of what parents should be, usually based on experiences and the media. (Cliff Huxtable and Ward Cleaver are not easy models to live up to.) When they compare their own parents to that ideal, their parents come up short. In short, they are already wrecks about their own behaviors and now have to deal with unpredictable and potentially geeky parents—no wonder they are embarrassed to be seen with us.

*What should parents do?* Such behavior usually peaks during middle school and early high school, and then diminishes by the junior or senior year. Respect the fact that teens are not always going to want to be seen with you and certainly not with their entire family. Go out with them one-on-one; taking everyone in the family on an outing is frequently a recipe for disaster. When you're out together, just have fun. Don't use the excursion as a time to set them straight on something. They'll see the ambush coming and will retreat.

## FAMILY TIME

> My mom and I go to horse shows together, so we need to learn how to get along.
> I went to Valley Fair with my family and we laughed and laughed.

Not spending time with the family is a frequent complaint expressed by parents about teenagers. Surprisingly, this is a cloud with a silver lining. A lack of family companionship is actually beneficial in helping teenagers achieve one of their major jobs during adolescence—autonomy. Teenagers are in the process of separating from the family and becoming their own person. They spend the majority of their time at school, with peers, and working jobs, all in an effort to grow up. As with everything, of course, moderation is important. Balancing inclusion and separation requires delicacy.

*What should parents do?* The times they are a-changin' and parents need to change with them. This situation is another one of the many instances in which adults need to give more than they receive. Try to be home when they are home, and work around their schedule. This is a real shift for parents; up until now, the child has worked around the adults' timetable. Your social life may suffer, you may have to shuffle some commitments, but it's important for the teen that you be available. A careful balance needs to be attained between family time, friend time, and alone time. In dysfunctional families, teens often try to get away from parental influence too early and become too peer dependent.

Do negotiate some family time because it's good for everyone to be together sometimes. And keep your eye on the bigger picture—do they spend their free time in healthy ways? If they participate in extracurricular or religious activities, hold down a job, or spend time with nice friends, support this behavior and do not consider it a negative.

## LAZINESS

On weekends, if I don't have anything to do, I just want to sleep until noon and then be on the computer.

Sound familiar? Teens can lounge around for unbelievable amounts of time just stewing in their own thoughts. Everyone else is cleaning, cooking, and running errands, but not them; they seem content to just sit. Our first reaction to their lethargic ways is frustration and dismay, but neuroscience is shedding new light on the subject. It seems that their brains are the reason for their lack of giddy-up-and-go. Teens have an underactive ventral striatal circuit, which is the part of the brain involved in motivation. Adolescents are pretty much wired as couch potatoes.

*What should parents do?* This is a point of understanding and tolerance. Take comfort in knowing that this too will pass.

## MESSY ROOMS

Teens and parents commonly fight about the state of the teenage bedroom. Littered with clothes, wires leading nowhere and everywhere, and the slight smell of rotting pizza represent a fairly typical picture. This state of affairs is enough to try the patience of the most understanding parents.

*What should parents do?* The best advice came from a grand-mother who said, "Keep the door shut. Just let them have their room." You don't have to tolerate their messiness in the rest of the house, but let their bedroom be their bastion. A messy bedroom is not the battlefield to die on; if you're not careful, it is a war you could wage on a daily basis.

You can, however, impose a few rules. If laundry isn't taken regularly to the laundry room, introduce them to the washer and dryer and teach them how to use it. Collect dirty plates and uneaten food once or twice a week (judge your own tolerance on this one) and have teens wash and put them away.

Another issue regarding teens and their bedrooms is privacy. An unwanted visit will be interpreted as a raid on their inner sanctum. With all the physical and mental changes going on in their brain, they would benefit (if possible) by having their own room.

## MAKING DECISIONS

I got embarrassed during class and I left school.
I tried a cigarette; my parents still don't know.
I squealed out of the parking lot and there was a cop right there.

Teens are known for making bad decisions, but they need to hone the decision-making skill. Decision making is one skill that requires careful negotiation in the fully developed frontal lobes. The brain of an early adolescent differs greatly from a late adolescent in anatomy, biochemistry, and physiology. At this age, the frontal lobes really can't tell the difference between a good decision and a bad decision.

*What should parents do?* Some parents have difficulty giving up control, often with the best of intentions, out of concern for their child's safety. Parents need to loosen the reins and let teens start making their own decisions and living with the consequences (still, keep the safety net handy). The old adage "Practice makes perfect" is the conventional wisdom that helps us keep perspective. Young teens should have a say in the clothes they wear (fortunately, school dress codes help limit the choices), who their friends are, and where and when they study (as long as they study). Older adolescents need to begin to make bigger decisions, such as how they spend their money, when they go to bed, and planning for their future.

## MORAL DEVELOPMENT

Older teenagers are ready to tackle complex moral dilemmas. They approach problems systematically and realize that two rules might conflict, that things aren't always black and white. Moral decisions engage many parts of the brain—long-term memories, emotional memories, visual and auditory memories, and the frontal lobes

Consider this dilemma: A favorite brother wants to borrow money from you, but you know he is a compulsive gambler. In three years he has gone through a million dollars. His marriage is on the rocks, as is his relationship with his only child, a seventeen-year-old daughter. He wants money to help pay for her college education.

At least twenty brain structures would apply themselves to this problem. Long-term memories (stored in the cerebral cortex) recall the many good times and talks you've enjoyed with your brother, as well as your conversation about his wife's chronic kidney disease, and make you feel sorry for him and his family.

Sympathy gets a boost from your visual cortex; the amygdala processes your brother's facial expressions and his embarrassment over his need for money. The amygdala also brings about a twinge of fear—if you turn him down, what will this do to your relationship with your brother or to your niece's future? Your ambivalence activates your premotor cortex, which rehearses throttling him. At the same time, your frontal lobe keeps you calm. The problem-solving function of this structure says some addictions are untreatable, and suggests that you might just as well give him the money and keep his affection. At this point, your frontal lobes steps in to take command and decides how to gently tell him no (but if you are financially secure, perhaps you will directly help your niece with her education).

*What should parents do?* Teenagers need their space to consider moral issues, and they also need opportunities to discuss moral issues with parents, peers, and teachers. The school, religious affiliation, and family are all places conducive to encouraging varied views and dynamic discussions in a safe environment. Moral development doesn't occur automatically; adolescents need to be challenged with various problems, wrestle with a variety of solutions, and sort out their views. Sensitivity to minorities, sexual harassment, and to those with special needs can be developed through education and experiences with diverse populations.

Getting involved in the community is a good way to create awareness of issues and at the same time allow the adolescent to make meaningful contributions to the well-being of others. Ultimately, moral development takes the energy and commitment of action as well as thought.

## WORK

The number of teens holding jobs has increased dramatically in the past two decades. Joining the work force is a source for independence and exploration, both tasks of adolescent development. Working ten hours or fewer per week during high school has been found to have advantages for teens; it teaches them responsibility, time management, and gives them spending money. Working more than twenty hours a week has been found to be detrimental to the teen; they miss extracurricular activities, it interferes with friend-ships, and academics suffer.

*What should parents do?* Allow your high school teenager to get a job, and then let them own it. Getting to work on time and han-dling issues as they come up should be their responsibility, not yours—although if they solicit your advice on a work-related prob-lem, it's perfectly acceptable to give a little expert advice. Also, curb the hours they are allowed to work. Discourage teens from working more than fifteen hours a week. Investing in a too-expensive car and paying for gas and insurance puts the pressure on to work longer hours. The real price they pay for this choice is having less time for extracurricular activities and friends. This is too high a price to pay during adolescence.

## FAST FACTS (FOR GENDER DIFFERENCES)

- The male brain is larger than the female brain (males are physically larger).
- There is no difference in IQ between the sexes.
- Males have a larger motor part in their brain.
- Males perform better on visual-spatial tasks (the right hemi-sphere of their brains is more developed).
- Females perform better on language tasks (the left hemi-sphere of their brains is more developed).
- Girls' brains develop faster than boys (they hit puberty ear-lier).
- Girls have a thicker corpus callosum, the network between the two hemispheres. The thicker this is, the better commu-nication there is between the two hemispheres.
- The hypothalamus becomes bigger and thicker in boys than in girls during adolescence; it is a part of the brain associated with sexual interest.

**⑩**

# TECHNOLOGY: THE MEDIUM
# AND THE MESSAGE

The only thing keeping up with the rapid changes going on in the teenage brain are the rapid changes in cyberspace. Thanks to all of the new technology now available, teens are creating brains quite different from those of their parents and grandparents. The digital world is creating digital brains and there are no boundaries to this new frontier.

## PUTTING THE PUZZLE TOGETHER

Did you know . . .

- . . . computer games emphasize quick, rapid responses in the teen's brain instead of encouraging thoughtful decisions?
- . . . watching television is a passive activity that does little to stimulate the brain?
- . . . daydreaming is counterproductive to building a better brain?
- . . . multitasking disrupts the brain?

The technology revolution is electrifying the globe and teens are confidently in charge. They are drawn like bees to honey toward this world of electrical routers, modems, and interconnections in cyberspace. Teens spend approximately six and a half hours a day hooked to the Internet. Their vocabularies are sprinkled with words like "instant messaging," "blogs," "MySpace," "YouTube," and "Facebook." In their minds, the networking possibilities are endless. The Internet is a way to entertain yourself, share ideas, look for a job, get a date, or seek advice. It's like an information shopping mall that never closes. You can shop online without ever leaving the house. On e-Bay, you can get a great pair of Birkenstocks for half price while you amuse yourself in a bidding war. But is all of this technology saving time or wasting time?

It's a new world for adults who grew up with no computer at home and only three television channels. My grandma's phone was a party line, and now my children feel lost if their cell phone isn't charged. When I told my daughter that one of my plans for this upcoming year was to expand my CD collection, she looked at me laughing and said, "Mom, CDs are out—everybody's using iPods." Just when I think I'm catching up, I find I'm one step behind.

No wonder it's easy for parents to drop the proverbial technoball without even realizing it was in play. We can no longer dip our toes into the cyberpool; we need to jump in, get wet, and at least start treading water. It's apparent that these technological innovations are life altering. Our kids have a wealth of knowledge at their fingertips, and they can communicate across oceans with a touch of a button—but these advancements also bring real concerns.

Granted, every mass communication medium has been viewed as a threat to young people by the older generation. I remember my grandparents not allowing a television set in their home for years, believing it too worldly. When Grandpa finally did break down and buy one, the general family consensus was that watching baseball on television just made good sense.

Whether it was comics, telephones, movies, radio, television, video games, or the Internet, media has always been assumed to have captivated the younger generation with a level of passive engagement that is close to addiction. Then the new medium weaves a dicey web around them by fascinating and entangling them with inappropriate content. Older generations worry that new media corrupt values and waste precious time that could be spent on studies or chores. These are in part valid concerns. Face it, when teens have a choice between doing homework, shooting the breeze with Dad, or playing on the Internet, the Internet usually wins.

## THE MESSAGE

Content does make a difference. This is not just common sense anymore; the American Psychological Association, the National Institutes of Health, the Surgeon-General's Office, the American Academy of Pediatrics, and the American Medical Association all endorse the fact that media violence influences youth aggression. Researchers have found disturbing evidence concerning teens and violent video games. Typically, video games require reflexive *reactions*—not reflective *responses*. These games stimulate the amygdala and neutralize the frontal lobes. Teens who engage in excessive violent video play have underactive frontal lobes during and long after the game has been unplugged. This means logical, reasonable thinking is muffled and fast reactive thinking is stimulated—and this plays out in everyday life. Instead of carefully deciding that they should get all of their equipment ready for band and leave for practice with an appropriate amount of time to park and get inside, teens find themselves shopping at the mall until ten minutes before band rehearsal, driving like a maniac through traffic, and then surprised when they get an expensive speeding ticket.

Additionally, games that are violent in nature trigger testosterone to be released into the system, further agitating the amygdala. A fury of emotions brews in their brains. Why else would a fifteen-year-old yell and slam his fist when you interrupt his Mortal Combat computer game?

Bruce Bartholow, a psychologist at the University of Missouri, says there are hundreds of studies that show people who are exposed to media violence become more aggressive. Very disturbing was his latest research that showed violent games made people indifferent to brutality. Young men who played a great deal of violent video games were shown pictures of violent crimes while fMRI scans were made of their brains. Their brains showed little reaction to the violence because they had been anesthetized to the "virtual" bloodshed.

## COMPUTER AND VIDEO GAMES

The controversy over these games spans a wide range of issues. Some people believe that the real problem with computer games is not the aggression but rather the damage the games cause by stunting the developing mind. Instead of spending time on academics, kids are playing video games. With lots of practice, they hone these video skills and their brains strengthen in this area, at the expense of expanding brain power in reading, writing, and math. Adolescence is a second chance to create a brain, and a steady diet of playing video and computer games neglects or redirects that potential.

The debilitating effect of video games was made clear with a study involving Nintendo. Teenagers playing a Nintendo game were compared to teens doing a simple, repetitive arithmetic problem. Scientists found the computer game only stimulated activity in the parts of the brain associated with vision and movement. Arithmetic, even simple arithmetic, stimulated brain activity in both the left and right hemispheres of the frontal lobe—the area most associated with learning, memory, and emotion. The students playing the computer games were actually halting the process of brain development. The message was that students need to read literature, compute math, interact with their environment, and communicate with peers to really develop a better brain.

Video games aren't the only negative influence on teens. Adolescents use television and print media mainly to support their interests in sports, world events, role models, and body image. Some of these messages are positive, some are not. It's self-evident that we are all affected by advertising—we always have been—but with new technology, this propaganda is able to spread at unprecedented rates and infiltrate every pore of the impressionable teenager. Three-quarters of teens say that they are influenced by the sexual behavior displayed in the media. When asked, adolescents expressed a preference for the beer made by the brewery with the largest advertising budget. The message matters.

## E-MAILS, INSTANT MESSAGING, CHAT ROOMS, AND BLOGS

But this concern with content doesn't tell the entire story about how technology can be troublesome; the very medium in which this content appears is potentially a problem. "I love IM [instant messaging]. I'm always on the computer, chatting with friends and going on MySpace. I've been on with at least three friends at one time. I'm on the phone, watching TV, eating ice cream, and IM[ing]." Another boy bragged that he had talked to up to twelve people at one time while listening to music and surfing the Web. The only problem he saw was that "Sometimes people get off before I can get back to them."

The Internet has changed the way education, industry, and governments do business. Few things bring out as much enthusiasm as instant messaging. Teenagers bubble over with comments about it like "I loooooove it," "It's addictive," "Even when I'm not supposed to, I constantly check my e-mail." Instant messaging has become a social hub for teenagers. It allows them to keep in contact with close and not-so-close friends without leaving the house. As long as it's not used in excess but is used as a vehicle for communication with friends, it's a wonderful invention.

On the other hand, potentially problematic is participation in chat rooms. Lonely, naïve kids e-mail and go to chat rooms with strangers, believing them to be friends who are always available and always understand them. Cyberstalkers prey on such immature kids and talk them into face-to-face meetings. The news periodically reports incidents of twelve- and thirteen-year-olds being lured to board buses and travel to distant hotels to meet their "friend." One teenage boy was coerced into posting a naked picture of himself on his computer, thinking it was for a fifteen-year-old girl. It doesn't take a brain scientist to suspect the unlikelihood that a fifteen-year-old girl put out that request; more likely it was a forty-year-old pedophile

Over half of all blogs (short for "Web log") are maintained by teenagers. Many use it as a way to journal and share their innermost thoughts. The main purpose seems to be to connect with their peers. This is probably an effective way to keep in touch with a variety of people at once. Instead of writing numerous e-mails about the school lunch menu and your plans for Friday night, you can just post your thoughts for all your friends to read. The problem is that not just friends can read your blog. Most kids who create blogs change their names as a security measure (or for the fun of having an alter ego), but usually the pseudonyms are so similar to their real names that it wouldn't take a detective to decipher their true identities. Naïve teens will go so far as to post their e-mail address, home address, phone number, or school, which puts them in danger of predators. And then there's the concern with what they actually say. Many teens reveal their most personal thoughts on their blog. After all, blogs are thought to be impenetrable because you need a password to reach the site, right?

Wrong. If one friend gives a password to another person, everyone that person is in contact with now also knows his or her blog password.

Nothing posted online can be considered "safe." Kids don't realize that once they post personal information on the Internet, it is potentially there forever. Even if they remove it twenty-four hours later, it is possible that it was saved somewhere and will reappear later, much to their chagrin. Even employers now check places like Facebook to see what job applicants have posted about themselves! A lack of discretion can come back to haunt adolescents in many different ways.

A group of English teachers I know are becoming concerned with the lack of proper English being used on instant messenger programs, in e-mails, and in blogs. The lack of correct grammar and sentence structure, and the abundance of abbreviations (for example, LOL for "laughing out loud") are being carried into the classroom. Grammar and punctuation rules are lost in the technodust.

Teens are also disadvantaging themselves as they multitask, switching between regular and Internet activities. While they are doing homework, they are also attempting to instant message and download songs. David Meyer, a psychologist who directs the Brain, Cognition, and Action Laboratory at the University of Michigan, says that the problem with multitasking is the time needed for reorientation after each interruption. Homework can take between 25 and 400 percent longer if you multitask (depending on the complexity and similarity of the tasks).

Working on two related tasks has the worst effect on thinking efficiency because they tap into the same parts of the brain. It's better to switch between math and piano than history and English. That's why you can easily fold laundry while listening to the stock market report—dissimilar tasks use two different parts of the brain.

## CELL PHONES

But computers are not the only modern problem parents grew up without facing. Cell phones are another good example of good and bad effects in one device. More than 500 million people in the world today use cell phones. They help us keep track of each other at the mall, have saved lives in snowstorms, and can take that once-in-a-lifetime photo of Bono in concert. But they have also been known to spread compromising pictures, assist in cheating on tests (via text messaging), and emit electromagnetic fields that excite the cortex with potential implications for epilepsy and other neurological conditions.

The problem of multitasking approaches life-and-death significance with the use of cell phones while driving. It is the activity of intense conversation that causes the problem, not the cell phone per se. The problem with cell phones is that when we drive we naturally silently talk to ourselves about driving while simultaneously using that same part of the brain to talk on the cell phone. It's a recipe for disaster. It's well-documented that drivers who talk on a cell phone are prone to accidents, just as those who drink and drive.

## WHAT PARENTS SHOULD DO

En masse, teens have immersed themselves in the digital world with all its exciting discoveries and innovations. Never has there been so much intermingling of potential and peril. The first thing parents need to do is identify which activities are problems and which are not. Eliminating all technology is not the solution. It would be commensurate with throwing down the gauntlet and challenging your teenager to a fight to the death. Besides, technology has many academic and social benefits when used responsibly.

Moderation is key when it comes to technology. Before you go ballistic, make small steps and keep the doors of communication open. Set reasonable limits on computer and television time and ask for your teen's input about these limits. Insist that homework be done before they log on to instant message or surf the Web. Turn off the television during meal times. Look at consumer ratings and use your own judgment to get an idea of what is appropriate content on television, in video games, and in magazines. Eliminate the violent video games, particularly for the young adolescent.

Keep technology out of their bedrooms. Privacy for using the computer is neither acceptable nor desirable. Keeping computer screens and television channel choices in public view keeps everyone honest. Outlaw talking on cell phones while driving, and suggest instead your teen pull over to make or take a phone call if it can't wait until she gets to her destination. Forbid young adolescents and discourage older adolescents from entering chat rooms with people they don't know and make it clear that strangers are not friends.

Clues that adolescents are in technology trouble can be found when they break family rules limiting the amount of technology use or sneak around to use it. Other signs of concern would be when they choose video games and instant messaging over getting together with friends in real life, doing homework, or sleeping, or become furious when asked to stop.

## FAST FACTS

- Seventy-eight percent of teens use computers at home.
- Ninety-five percent of teens use computers at school on a regular basis.
- Seventy-three percent of teens use the Internet regularly.

- Ninety percent of teens play video games regularly.
- Only five hours per week of playing violent video games will show brain activity with aggressive thoughts.
- Watching an excessive amount of television has been associated with obesity in girls.

**II**

# TEENS AT RISK

**R**ebels without a clue. All teenagers have some residue of rebellion and at-risk behavior lurking in their psyche, but a few teens drive in the fast lane and make choices that will haunt them for a lifetime. Parents, schools, and the judicial system try desperately to guide and shelter these teens through the precarious years of adolescence. Now neuroscientists are joining the effort. They are hopeful that their research will lead to better understanding and help for troubled teens.

## PUTTING THE PUZZLE TOGETHER

Did you know . . .

- . . . teens are drawn to risky behavior?
- . . . teenagers are very vulnerable to addictions?
- . . . teenage girls' brains are more traumatized by alcohol than boys'?

- . . . the United States was one of the last countries in the world to prohibit capital punishment for crimes committed by juveniles?

Teenagers who find themselves in a severe depression, addicted to drugs, or in trouble with the law can bring their parents to their knees. There is almost nothing parents won't do for their children, but sometimes it is difficult for them to sort out what to do and when. What is a legitimate concern and what is needless worry? One of the most proactive things parents can do is to learn the facts about teenage at-risk behavior. In this case, knowledge breeds understanding and comfort.

"At risk" describes a big continuum of behaviors. At one end is the normal exploration teenagers often dapple in—trying a cigarette ("Do I look cool?"), speeding down I-90 ("I'll never get caught"), or attempting to buy soft pornography. I'm not saying that parents should approve these activities, but just as there is a difference between catching a cold and catching AIDS, there is a difference between the behavior and exploration of the "normal" teen and the at-risk teen. A small percentage of teens fall into the category of at risk, and their changing brains make them more likely to make unhealthy decisions and engage in risky behavior.

The following are danger signs that teens are at risk:

- Isolation from family and friends
- Sudden changes in schoolwork, job performance, or athletic activities
- Drastic mood swings
- Lack of interest in outside school activities
- Family conflict
- Living in a community with high crime and easy availability of alcohol and drugs
- Delinquent friends
- Academic failure

- Change in eating and sleeping habits
- Cutting or hurting themselves

## ALCOHOL, DRUGS, AND SMOKING

"I was part of the subculture, very common to be drinking and doing pot. There was always somebody stoned or drunk," said one teen. Another said, "Everybody drinks, it's the norm, it's just expected. Every weekend we get together and drink. One time it's at one kid's house, the next time at somebody else's."

A person can sink into the deep abyss of addiction at any age, but it is particularly easy to do so during adolescence. Environment (stress from school, peers, or parents), personal genetics (the grandfather and an aunt were alcoholics), and the brain all contribute to addiction susceptibility. During the teen years, there is a window of sensitivity to addiction, which means if the brain is exposed to something addictive it will have a more serious and detrimental effect than at other times. The teenage brain that is exposed to addictive substances will have a greater likelihood of becoming addicted quickly and staying addicted. Neuroscientists speculate that this is due to the complex changes that are occurring in their brain.

Alcohol and other addictive substances follow a common course in the brain. For immediate purposes, I'll use alcohol as an example. Alcohol supplies people with a dopamine rush, which means that when you have a glass of wine or a mug of beer, you feel good, you relax. Unfortunately, as the brain receives more and more dopamine with regular drinking, it is fooled into believing it doesn't need to naturally produce as much. People who become addicted to alcohol and other drugs have a limited natural production of dopamine and therefore don't feel the natural highs (getting an A on a report card or seeing the school win the football game) that others do. Their bodies have downsized the reservoir, resulting in the need to drink more in order to feel joy.

The frontal lobes and hippocampus are particularly vulnerable to addiction. The hippocampus shrinks with excessive drinking, which limits short-term memory. Teens addicted to alcohol can't remember very well what they did the night before, whom they were with, and where they went. It is thought that one binge-drinking episode can impair a teen's memory for thirty days. For an entire month, a teen will not learn as much in school as he or she might have without drinking. Fortunately, short-term memory is very resilient and, when drinking stops, it will eventually restore to normal.

The frontal lobes, which are in charge of making good decisions, are quickly affected by drinking. The ability to make good choices is tenuous at best during adolescence, but under the influence of alcohol teens make decisions with carefree abandon. People of any age become less inhibited when they drink (you've seen them at karaoke night), but teens become particularly uninhibited. This puts them at risk for engaging in sexual activity, fighting, and pursuing dangerous activities that they would probably not consider if they were not intoxicated.

One sixteen-year-old girl, who abstained from drinking, routinely found herself the designated driver. "Everybody would drink too much and then we'd get into cars and go crazy. Every time we came to a stop sign or a bridge, everybody would yell 'stop sign' or 'bridge,' whoever yelled last had to take off some of their clothes—shirts, camis were flying. Everybody just thought it was fun, nobody was embarrassed, not even the next day." This story is evidence that good decision making was not part of the fun.

The problems with drinking don't stop at decision making. Teens' bodies don't manifest the physical signs that they have drunk too much as soon as adults' bodies do. Adults slow down and become sleepy, start slurring their words, and lose the ability to walk straight when they overindulge. Teens will eventually get these same signals, but they happen much later. Without these warning signs, they continue to drink until they are very, very drunk.

Finally, once an addiction is in place, the teenage brain is very resistant to treatment. The statistics for recovery from any addiction are grim at best, but for the teenager the fight becomes a lifelong battle.

Addiction issues may be particularly compounded for girls. Recent research shows that teenage girls are even more vulnerable to alcohol's effects than are boys. Girls who continually drink are at increased risk for behavioral problems and more neural abnormalities than boys.

Although it seems like a less dangerous addiction (although not necessarily less physically harmful), smoking is another problem that starts in adolescence. About 90 percent of smokers had their first cigarette before they were twenty-one years old. Like other substance addictions, smoking is hard-wired into the adolescent brain and follows the same path of quick addiction and resistance to treatment. One seventeen-year-old confessed, "I am so addicted that I even smoke in the shower."

Preliminary research with rats found that mothers who smoked exposed their unborn pups to nicotine and altered the brain structures and brain cell activity in regions crucial to learning, memory, and reward. These changes subsequently influenced nicotine's effects on their offspring during adolescence—a time when people often choose to begin smoking. Teens whose mothers smoked during pregnancy can show signs of nicotine dependence and withdrawal after just a handful of cigarettes. The home environment is not what makes a child prone to a cigarette addiction, and it does not matter if the mother continued to smoke once the child was born (although the potential availability of cigarettes and parental modeling may influence a teen's willingness to try smoking in the first place). The damage done during the prenatal period makes teenagers vulnerable to nicotine addiction. And, just as with drugs and alcohol, teen brains are hard-wired to the addiction, making quitting a grueling affair.

*What should parents do?* First, don't overreact if you catch your teen with alcohol or cigarettes. Lecturing, nagging, and threatening do not work. Instead, be a good role model. Do not smoke and limit or eliminate drinking in front of your teenager. Don't stockpile liquor or cigarettes in your home; this helps curb the temptation. Maintain a sensible perspective. It is one thing to allow your teenager to have a sip of wine at home and another to become intoxicated with your teen—clearly make the distinction. If you are or have been addicted to drinking or smoking, talk to your teen about it. Tell him or her about how you became addicted, the impact of the addiction on your life, and what you are doing to quit the habit. Then connect your teen with a support group such as Al-Anon or Alateen.

Do not leave your teen unsupervised for long periods of time and definitely do not leave him or her alone overnight. Unsupervised nights set teens up for trouble. The teenage brain and its teenage friends are not prepared to handle this much responsibility.

If your teen arrives at home and it's evident he has been drinking, don't try to talk about it at that moment. Instead, send him directly to bed, and talk the next day. No one is in shape for a productive discussion when he or she is under the influence.

Drinking and driving is non-negotiable, as is riding with a friend who has been drinking. If the teenager does end up drinking with friends, have a prenegotiated deal with her to call home for a ride. If she holds up her end of the bargain by calling for a ride, waive the consequences (at least the first time). One bad choice should not end up as a deadly decision.

If there is an alcohol- or drug-related tragedy at school or in the community, do not use it as an opportunity to lecture your teen on the dangers of substance use. Doing so overrides your teenager's chance to mourn and learn from the heartbreak. Instead, listen to

his thoughts and encourage him to talk about it. Allow him to draw
his own meaningful conclusions.

The teenager with an addiction problem needs treatment and
the sooner the better. Before admitting your teenager to a treatment facility, take the time to check out the program. Consider the
following:

- Juveniles and adults should not be placed together.
- The program should offer group and individual counseling
  with frequent treatment schedules.
- The percentage of recovery.
- The percentage of certified staff.
- Whether the program offers continued professional support
  once a patient leaves the facility.

## ANGER AND AGGRESSION

Teenagers are naturally drawn to wild and crazy things and they
are more impulsive and rash than adults. Rubin Gur, a professor of
psychology and the director of the Brain Behavior laboratory at the
University of Pennsylvania, says that of all the emotions, impulse
control is the last to develop (which should come as no surprise to
parents or middle and high school teachers).

The teenage propensity to take risks comes from a variety of
sources, including trying to impress peers, an indestructible belief
about themselves, and the changes in their brains. Novelty and
danger are a tantalizing concoction. They stimulate dopamine production and, in combination, create the same rush that drugs like
crack and meth generate. Add to this a lack of impulse control and
aggressive behavior is spawned.

There appear to be gender differences with aggression just as
there are with the effects of alcohol, but with aggression boys are
the ones at greater risk. Research studies have noted a male child

is six times more likely than a female child to be identified as having aggressive behavior that disrupts his life. Aggressive behaviors exhibited by boys can be attributed to several things, including biology, cultural differences, learning style, the structure of the classroom, the acceptance of the nurturing adult, and the brain.

The amygdala, the emotional center of the brain, is heavily involved in aggressive behavior. It remains in control throughout most of adolescence even as the logical reasoning area of the brain steadily and optimistically vies for power. By later adolescence, the frontal lobes are winning the game and self-control is improving, but until then the amygdala is in control. The impact of the amygdala on aggression was shown in a study of monkeys that had their amygdalas removed, which made them quite docile and passive. Other studies showed that when monkeys' amygdalas were electrically stimulated, the animals became more violent.

A major stimulant to the amygdala in boys is the male hormone testosterone. Males with higher testosterone levels tend to be more socially aggressive but not more violent. Although an aggressive predisposition is usually destructive, it can be directed in a positive manner. CEOs, professional athletes, and high-ranking politicians often have elevated levels of testosterone, which seems to benefit their careers.

Contributing to aggression is the fact that serotonin, a calming neurotransmitter, is released at a lower rate in teens' brains, just when it could be of the most use. Fortunately, positive social feedback ("Good work" and "I like how you handled that") from a significant adult (like Mom or Dad) has been shown to increase serotonin levels in the brain.

*What should parents do?* Listen to what teens say and focus on their feelings. Blaming them and accusing them of acting inappropriately is only going to increase the anger and shut down any chances of communication. Stick to facts during confrontations and try to reduce high emotions. If your teen loses control, you should stay calm; they need firm, consistent reactions.

When things have cooled down, discuss appropriate ways to handle an insult or threat. Often a warning and discussion is all they need. If they continue to show anger and act aggressively, take away privileges—but not the one activity that they love best. That extracurricular activity or friendship may be the one and only thing that helps them control their emotions; without it, they could flounder.

Also, be a good role model. Let your teen see how you maturely handle the frustration of a two-hour computer breakdown or an uncooperative service man. People learn by example and your teen is always watching you. Finally, keep him or her busy with extracurricular activities, service clubs, and hobbies. The more supervised a teen is, the less likely he or she is to exhibit inappropriate behaviors. Teenagers who are persistently aggressive may need to attend anger management classes to learn to control their emotions. Refer to strategies for parents included in the section on ADHD.

Signs of teenage aggression may be:

- Resisting authority
- Being disrespectful of others
- Relying on aggression to solve problems
- Mediocre or worse academic work
- Cutting classes, getting suspended, or dropping out
- Gang involvement
- Alcohol or drug use

## ADHD (ATTENTION DEFICIT HYPERACTIVITY DISORDER)

He has a different group of friends every week and he's always in trouble at school—blurts out answers, argues with his teachers. This is the second time he's taken freshman English—he doesn't focus unless he's playing a video game and you can forget about him turning in homework. His mom and I are worried sick. We're thinking of sending him to an alternative school next year, he's got to graduate. (Words from a discouraged father, as he describes his tenth-grade son with ADHD.)

Imagine every aggravating, normal teenage tendency—impulsivity, risk taking, argumentativeness. Now multiply that by 100 and you have a teenager with ADHD.

Due to a short attention span, anyone with ADHD struggles with the concept of time and sequencing. This becomes a real problem during the teen years when the expectation is that you are old enough to manage your own time. If the ADHD teen is told to be home by 10:00 P.M., it is not uncommon for her to show up two or three hours late. The reason is tied much more to her ADHD than to disobedience. She is busy playing computer games, skateboarding, and listening to music and the last thing she is paying attention to is the time. And to top it off, these teens have difficulty understanding sequencing and its cause-and-effect nature. They are grounded for being home late, but continue to break curfew, not comprehending that the reason for the grounding is the fact they are home late.

Grappling with sequencing makes it difficult for them to get away with anything. They drink part of your bottle of wine and when you confront them about it, they are surprised. How did you know? It never dawns on them that since over half the bottle of wine is gone, and no adult in the family drank it, that it's only a small leap in thought to suspect the teen. Hence, being sneaky is not their strength.

"I don't know" is a constant mantra of the ADHD teenager. Part of this stems from problems with sequencing and part of it comes from not focusing on anything for an extended period of time. You ask him to take out the garbage, he starts to take it out, gets distracted by a phone call, decides to let the dog out, plays with the dog a bit, and looks for that CD he's been missing. Thirty minutes have passed since you asked him to take the garbage out and it is still in the wastebasket. When you ask him, "Why haven't you taken out the garbage?" The answer is a sincere "I don't know." And they don't. The road to a straight answer has been convoluted by a crooked array of activities.

It's also common for them to focus on one activity to the distraction of all others. They are instant messaging and fail to notice that they have been called for dinner ten times. This hyperfocusing is most common in activities like computer games and instant messaging—things that constantly require their focus and response. Interrupting ADHD teens who are hyperfocusing will always cause an outburst. They are expending a great deal of energy on one task and an interruption carries them beyond their level of frustration. As a parent, you will feel their wrath. Once provoked, ADHD teenagers are usually more argumentative and aggressive than other teens. They quickly go out of control and have a difficult time settling down afterward.

There is clear evidence that there is a biological difference between the brains of ADHD individuals and others. This proof, from the world of neuroscience, should help take the blame off parents and ADHD teenagers for their inappropriate behavior. For many years it was thought that if parents would just lay down the law or if the teenager would just pay attention, all the nonsense would stop. Now we know better.

There are abnormalities in many parts of the brain, and some more significant than others. Children and teenagers with ADHD have slightly smaller brains, about 3–4% smaller (this is not due to taking hyperactivity drugs such as Ritalin, which was once theorized). The smaller the brain, the more significant the ADHD symptoms, but the size does not make a difference in intelligence.

The basal ganglia, a part of the brain involved in thinking and muscle control, has lower activity rates, as do areas in the frontal lobes. Not surprisingly, the areas in the frontal lobes that control attention and impulse are smaller in individuals with ADHD.

*What should parents do?* Stay calm and then stay clam again and expect overreactions with ADHD teenagers. When they explode, turn a deaf ear. It's not uncommon to have to turn this deaf ear for a one- or two-minute tirade. Do not get off topic. Do not defend yourself. These responses won't help your teenager get under control and will usually result in his or her behavior escalating. Your best bet is to wait and then simply restate your original request in a quiet and nonconfrontational tone.

If the outburst goes along the lines of "I don't see why I have to get off the computer; Lindsey never has to get off the computer," do not explain the computer rules to him; he is trying to bring you down to his level by engaging you in the argument. Instead turn the tables on him and say, "Why do you think we have those rules?" The typical response will be "I don't know." Reply with "Then tell me what you do know." Continue this same phrase in response to their "I don't know." About 80 percent of the time, they will explain the rule to you and in the process calm down.

The issue of medication is a weighty one. There is no doubt that there is currently significant abuse of hyperactive drugs. That being said, if a proper diagnosis has been made, medication should strongly be considered. The consequences of uncontrolled ADHD are life limiting. Teenagers with ADHD have high dropout rates, difficulty maintaining friendships, and frequently change jobs. If your teenager is on medication, realize that adjustments will probably be necessary with the physical changes that occur during puberty.

## LEGAL CULPABILITY

On March 1, 2005, the United States became one of the last countries in the world to prohibit capital punishment for crimes committed by juveniles. The Supreme Court referenced research findings by the American Psychological Association and the American Medical Association regarding the development of the adolescent brain as it relates to criminal culpability. The teenage frontal lobe was found to be lacking in the ability to foresee consequences, control impulses, and modify actions and responses. This information influenced the court's decision. Now it is decreed that even if teenagers commit adult crimes, because they are not equipped with an adult brain, they should not receive an adult punishment.

Teenagers tend to commit crimes on impulse, like theft and simple assault. Other crimes that juveniles are likely to carry out include arson, vandalism, and disorderly conduct. Such crimes contain an element of the rash decision making and reactive violence that diminishes as the brain reaches maturation. Drug crimes also make up a large amount of juvenile arrests, which reflects on the juveniles' inability to appropriately assess the long-term consequences of their actions.

If there is good news about teenage crime, it is this: Crimes that involve a greater amount of premeditation or malice are less prevalent among juveniles. Arrests of teenagers for violent crimes are relatively small. Painfully, 80 percent of teens who commit murder kill the person who is abusing their mother. Many juvenile offenders grow out of their criminal behavior and stop participating in criminal activities as they become adults.

*What should parents do?* If you believe your teenager is experimenting in risky business, get help for him or her before it becomes a legal issue. Seek assistance from counselors, social workers, religious organizations, and the schools. If your child is arrested, stay by his side and help him work it out—this is no time to abandon him. A good lawyer and counselor are an investment in his future, so get the best you can afford. The teen shouldn't feel alone—and neither should the parent.

## DEPRESSION AND SUICIDE

Reports of feeling "very happy" drop during the teen years. Adolescents have a more negative spirit until about age eighteen. They face more emotional turmoil and have a difficult time looking at life through rose-colored glasses. Although a subpositive disposition is the norm for most teenagers, in some it hits serious levels and depression sets in.

Most professionals believe that depression results from a combination of genetics, environment, and biology. It's been well documented that certain families have a history of depression that runs through generations. Environmental issues, such as physical and mental abuse, feelings of rejection, never being able to live up to parental expectations, and failure in school are also linked to depression. Even breaking up with a girl or boyfriend, a natural and normal part of growing up, can be seen as the end of the world and lead to a serious depression for a teenager.

Puberty, a natural physical development, also seems to play a role in teenage depression. The National Institutes of Health stated that there is a connection between puberty and depression. They found that as a person progresses through puberty, depression increases. In fact, progression through puberty is a more accurate predictor of depression onset than chronological age. Progesterone puts girls at an even higher risk. Once progesterone is released into the system, it allows cortisol, the stress hormone, to run rampant, which makes it very difficult for girls to restore their mental harmony.

Lower levels of serotonin during adolescence also contribute to depression. Normally serotonin inhibits the firing of neurons and makes us feel relaxed. It works as a check and balance with the emotional amygdala. For most teens, the drop in serotonin levels is not a problem, but for some teens it seems to increase the propensity for depression. There are two theories for why this happens. Some researchers speculate that some teens can't properly use the serotonin they have and others reason that the levels are so low that they are ineffective.

The right prefrontal cortex, which controls negative feelings, is dominant in depressed people and allows negative thoughts and memories to take control. Much like an annoying jingle you can't get out of your head, tape recordings of bad messages run over and over through depressed people's minds, sinking them further into despair. The hippocampus is also negatively affected. It decreases in size with chronic depression and its neurons begin to wither and die, which makes it difficult to remember old information (like happier times), process emotion, or learn anything new.

Severe depression may lead to thoughts of suicide or actual attempts to end one's life. Suicide is strongly correlated with depression and it is the third leading cause of death in teenagers. Very few suicide attempts are made before the age of fourteen, but between the age of fourteen and twenty-five, there is a dramatic increase in rates. The following are signs to watch for in teens who might be suicidal:

- Talking about suicide or death in general
- Talking about going away
- Giving away personal possessions
- Talking about feeling hopeless or guilty
- Withdrawing from friends and family
- Losing the desire to go out or take part in favorite activities
- Having trouble concentrating or thinking clearly
- Experiencing changes in eating or sleeping habits
- Weight loss
- Engaging in self-destructive behavior (drinking alcohol, taking drugs, or self-cutting)
- Poor school performance
- Depression
- Suffering a loss, like a death in the family or a breakup

- Sudden outbursts of temper
- Expressing a plan for suicide

What should parents do?

- Take warning signs seriously.
- Don't devalue their feelings by saying everything is okay.
- Communicate that you care and are listening.
- Be nonjudgmental.
- Directly ask teens hinting at suicide if they are planning to hurt themselves.
- Do not promise to keep conversations about suicidal intentions a secret.
- Seek professional help.
- Do not leave a suicidal teenager alone.

## ABUSED TEENS

Ongoing research suggests that the adolescent brain is far more dynamic and more susceptible to the effects of good and bad experiences than was previously thought. Electroencephalography (EEG) and fMRI imaging have provided neuroscientists with evidence that physical and sexual abuse that occurs during adolescence leaves scars in the adult brain. The left hemisphere of the brain, the limbic system, and the corpus callosum are particularly affected and show abnormal activity in abused people. In the real world, these individuals demonstrate more difficulty handling stress.

Researchers are now beginning to view the impact of verbal abuse on teenagers, too. The stress caused by repeatedly being exposed to cruel words is speculated to wound the brain.

*What should parents do?* If your son or daughter claims that he or she was abused, take your child seriously. If you don't believe her the first time she brings the subject up, she will never come to you again. If you suspect that abuse is happening, but your teen says nothing, directly ask her. Realize that she may not, out of shame or embarrassment, answer truthfully at first. Physical and sexual abuse is a life-altering and life-threatening experience that requires the aid of professionals; seek help from a trained therapist for diagnosis and treatment.

## STEROIDS

Every teenager wants to hit the tennis ball like Maria Sharapova, shoot a basket like LeBron James, and run for the goal like Shawn Alexander. Four to 6 percent of high school senior males and 1 to 3 percent of high school senior females have tried performance-enhancing steroids. Anabolic steroids are a synthetic form of the male hormone testosterone, which causes such things as a deepened voice and larger muscles. They give an athlete a decided advantage, and the fact that they are illegal and unfair in competition is often lost in the roaring cheer of the crowd.

Sadly, many teenagers feel the pressure to use steroids to keep up with their athletic peers. Steroids can increase the body's muscle tissue, but they may also cause sterility, stunted growth, and severe mood swings. Steroids activate the hypothalamus and other emotional areas of the brain and send out more aggressive signals, which may rouse long-term, negative emotions in teens. This dramatically shortens teenage fuses, making them *more* likely to argue with the coach, their teammates, or the referees. This hostile behavior may continue into young adulthood.

There is concern that steroids may change the brain's wiring for good. Teens who engage in this chemical abuse tend to use heavier steroids as they get older, which sets the stage for other illegal drug use. Steroid use has been linked to health problems such as heart attacks, stroke, and liver cancer.

*What should parents do?* The bulk of a teen's body should make steroid use fairly evident, but it you are unsure, speak to a professional about what signs to look for. Openly ask a teenager if he or she is taking steroids. Seek counseling and consider drug testing on a regular basis.

## CUTTING

> A group of us were at the beach and Beth was talking about a big fight she'd had with her mom and dad. Then Caroline said, "That is nothing compared to my family," and she pulled her swimsuit down and showed us where she had cut herself all around her bikini line and said, "This is what I do." She was just mutilated—it was gross. We all knew her mom was never around and had all kinds of different boyfriends that abused her—she didn't go into details, but she hinted. We told our parents and she went into treatment. (a twelve-year-old girl telling about the first time she realized that cutting was an option)

Cutting, a form of self-injury, is nothing new, but like so many dirty little secrets it's only now coming into the light of day. The majority of cutters are young girls between the ages of thirteen and fifteen. Usually they use a razor to cut the skin, causing bleeding, but not directly hitting a vein or artery that would be life threatening. The copycat nature of teenager behavior makes it a special concern for parents. Some educators have observed in school that some groups are anorexic and others are cutters.

Young teens use cutting as a means of handling strong emotion, as a way of relieving tension and stress. The issues that prompt cutting range from a young girl breaking up with a boyfriend and feeling that no one understands her to physical and emotional abuse. In the case of abuse, the pain of cutting takes away the numbness the teen feels in his or her life. Whatever the underlying cause, cutting is a way of speaking when no words will come. None of these teens have healthy coping skills. They don't have ways of dealing with intense emotions in an appropriate way.

Although the reason for cutting is environmental, the brain does become involved. Researchers have found that serotonin, a calming agent, is not properly used in the brains of these teens. It is also theorized that the cuts release endorphins, the body's natural painkillers, creating feelings of pleasure.

*What should parents do?* Be savvy. Most cutters feel shame and go to great lengths to hide their cuts. Take note if your teenager always wears long sleeves, even when it doesn't make sense, such as during hot weather or washing dishes. If she confesses to you about her cutting, validate her feelings. You don't have to approve of her behavior, but you do need to let her know that it's okay to feel upset, overwhelmed, or depressed.

It should come as no shock that teens look to technology for emotional support. There are many websites that give support to teens who cut. You may want to check out the website first, but don't be surprised if your teen finds meaningful connections there, and the sites are available twenty-four hours a day.

Be a good role model, and exhibit healthy ways of coping with stress and other high emotions (refer to coping skills in chapter 3). Consult a counselor or therapist. Hopefully, your teen will accompany you, but if not, go alone and perhaps you'll find ways to help both you and your teenager cope. There is preliminary research indicating that medications that reduce depression and anxiety may also help cutters; a therapist will be able to advise your teenager on this possibility.

If your teen needs medical services for physical injuries due to cutting, be his or her advocate. Some emergency room professions are not empathetic to wounds that are self-inflicted. Your teenager deserves the same attention, anesthesia, and respect as those with accidental inflictions.

## POVERTY

Poverty, violence, substance abuse, neglect, and sexual assault put teenagers in the at-risk column. Once one or more of these detrimental factors are part of a teenager's life, the probability of dropping out of school skyrockets. Dropouts are now a national problem and the numbers continue to rise.

Poverty undermines the quality and number of experiences an individual has in life, which reduces the amount of dendrites and synaptic connections in the brain. Children in poverty are probably not read to every night, not receiving the best daycare, and not playing on a home computer. Kids born into poverty miss an opportunity to increase their brain power right from birth. They enter kindergarten with vocabularies about half the size of the average five-year-old, and this deficiency shadows them into their teenage years.

Medical care, safety, nutrition, maternal depression, substance abuse, and violence are all ugly comrades of poverty. It's not surprising that researchers have found that the primary emotions found in teens living in poverty are fear and stress. Stress puts the brain on survival mode. It can no longer attend to issues like paying attention to the teacher or learning the connection between mitochondria and prokaryote because it is concentrating on the more important job of ensuring safety, health, and sustenance.

Unfortunately, fear of failure, isolation, and trauma—often present in teens living in poverty—causes dopamine to be converted into norepinephrine. Norepinephrine energizes an individual and, under adverse conditions, results in aggression and agitation.

Researchers have also found that individuals in poverty have less serotonin in their bodies, which contributes to feelings of unrest and anxiety. This makes it difficult for the individual to tolerate any additional frustration and stress in his or her life. Students may become argumentative or just give up when things get tough in school.

*What should parents do?* Poverty is a societal problem, but parents still have individual power. If you are in a temporary or permanent poverty situation, contact the schools or Social Services to see what help is available for your child. Factors that protect and improve resiliency to poverty include:

- A stable, positive, emotional relationship with at least one parent or responsible adult
- Average or above-average intelligence
- Past success to build a foundation for belief in future success
- Active coping, seeking to solve their own problems or overcome challenges
- A positive temperament (a largely inborn trait)—active and social, not passive and isolated
- An open and supportive educational and social climate at home and school
- Neighborhood and community support
- A sense of humor
- Caring for others
- Problem-solving skills
- The ability to find alternate solutions
- Critical reasoning skills
- High self-esteem
- Impulse control
- Planning ability
- Goal-setting capability

## FAST FACTS

- Forty percent of adolescent deaths are caused by vehicle accidents.
- Fifty percent of teens have tried drinking by age fourteen.
- Forty-two percent of teens have tried smoking by age fourteen.

- Teens have the highest rate of STDs of any age group.
- The U.S. teenage pregnancy rate is higher than in any other industrialized nation.
- Twenty to 30 percent of high school students consider suicide.
- Teens are more susceptible to stress than adults.
- The highest percentage of babies of teen mothers are born nine months after the prom; the second-highest percentage are born nine months after graduation.

## CONCLUSION

It is my firm conviction that the more we know about the inner ticking of the teenage brain, the better parents we will be. Thanks to a whole lot of neuroscientists who have expended a great deal of time and energy, more is now known about the teenage brain than ever before. Their discoveries are complementing the work of psychologists and educationists to give us a more complete and accurate view of the adolescent.

This knowledge will not ensure that we won't ever be frustrated or angry as parents. In fact, there is no doubt in my mind that a sense of humor is probably our best defense, followed by patience and tolerance. But there is comfort in familiarity. And the more familiar we become with the changes going on in the adolescent brain, the more comfortable we will be in guiding teenagers into adulthood.

# PARENTING GLOSSARY

**Abstinence.** Voluntary denial of sex of any kind

**Acne.** Inflamed skin glands often caused by hormone changes during puberty

**Addiction.** Repeated use of substances or behaviors that are harmful

**ADHD.** Attention deficit hyperactivity disorder; a neurological disorder that involves hyperactivity, impulsivity, and an inability to focus

**Adolescence.** The transition between childhood and adulthood, eleven to nineteen years old

**Amygdala.** Part of the brain that processes and remembers emotions; it is involved in anger and fear

**Anorexia.** Eating disorder that involves self-starvation; anorexics turn away from food to control their lives

**At risk.** Threat of dropping out of school

**Attachment disorder.** Normal attachment to parents does not occur within the first two years of life, resulting in multiple social and emotional problems

**Axon.** The part of the neuron that sends information to other neurons

**Basal ganglia.** Part of the brain associated with motor control, thinking, and emotion

**Binge drinking.** Four alcohol drinks for a woman and five for a man within a short period of time

**Bisexual.** Romantic or erotic desire for both men and women

**Blog.** A website created by an individual that journals his or her thoughts and interests

**Body language.** Communicating through body movements and gestures

**Brain.** Part of the central nervous system located in the skull; the region responsible for storing, organizing, and retrieving information

**Bulimia nervosa.** Eating disorder that involves binging on food and then purging; the bulimic turns to food to control his or her life

**Cerebellum.** The part of the brain in control of physical movement

**Chat room.** Live conversations with others via computers

**Chlamydia.** Sexually transmitted disease, it can cause sterility in women; males are carriers

**Clique.** A restricted social group

**Cognitive neuroscience.** The scientific study of the brain by neuroscientists, psychologists, and educationists

**Corpus callosum.** A network of neurons that connect the left and right hemispheres of the brain

**Cortisol.** Hormone released under stress; reduces the immune system and memory and increases blood pressure and heart rate

**Crush.** Short-lived feeling of affection for another person

**Dendrite.** Part of a neuron that receives messages from other neurons; one neuron may possess thousands of dendrites

**Depression.** A condition where an individual is sad, lethargic, and unmotivated

**Dopamine.** A neurotransmitter in the brain that makes a person feel good

**eBay.** An Internet company where people can buy and sell items

**EEG.** Electroencephalography; technology that measures electrical activity in the brain

**E-mail.** Sending messages to others on a computer via modem or telephone lines

**Endorphins.** Peptides that give a sense of well-being and reduced pain

**Estrogen.** A female hormone involved with menstruation, breast development, and pregnancy

**Facebook.** A social Internet site

**fMRI scans.** Functional magnetic resonance imaging; a brain imaging technology that examines the functions of the brain

**Frontal lobes.** A part of the brain involved in decision making, language, problem solving, planning, and controlling

**Gang.** A group of individuals who share common characteristics and engage in criminal activity

**Gay.** A homosexual male

**Heterosexual.** Physical, romantic, and spiritual attraction between individuals of opposite sexes

**Hippocampus.** A part of the brain associated with transferring short-term memories into long-term memory

**HIV/AIDS.** Disease that is transmitted through bodily fluids that attacks the immune system; there is no known cure

**Homosexual.** Physical, romantic, and spiritual attraction between individuals of the same sex

**Hypothalamus.** Part of the brain in control of pain, pleasure, hunger, thirst, and sexual desire

**Identity crisis.** The act of searching for and discovering your identity

**Identity.** A person's physical, sexual, vocational, and religious makeup

**Internet.** Interconnected computers throughout the world

**Leptin.** A hormone that regulates appetite and metabolism

**Lesbian.** A homosexual female

**Limbic system.** A part of the brain involved in emotion and emotional memories

**Melatonin.** Nature's sleeping pill released by the brain

**Menstruation.** The uterine wall of females sheds and bleeds approximately every twenty-eight days; this is often referred to as a period

**MP3 player.** A portable electronic device, such as an iPod, that stores and plays digital music

**Music downloading.** A song or album that can be copied off the Internet from such sites as iTunes, Napster, e-Music, etc.

**Myelination.** Insulates neurons so they can communicate more efficiently

**Neuron.** A brain cell; it consists of dendrites, axon, and a cell body

**Neuroscience.** Study of the nervous system and the brain

**Nocturnal emission.** Ejaculation during sleep, often referred to as a wet dream

**Norepinephrine.** A hormone that releases energy

**Obesity.** Overweight to the point of unhealthy

**Parietal lobes.** A part of the brain associated with touch, temperature, and pain

**Peer pressure.** A group of people who influence another person's actions or thoughts

**PET scans.** Positron emission tomography; a three-dimensional view of the brain that shows the structure and functions occurring in the brain

**Pruning.** Synaptic connections and dendrites are eliminated in the brain

**Puberty.** An individual becomes capable of reproduction

**Schizophrenia.** A mental disorder that impairs perceptions of reality; often occurs in late adolescence

**Search engines.** A website, such as Google, that can be used to search web pages across the Internet for a particular word or phrase

**Self-esteem.** A person's view of himself or herself; a positive or negative judgment

**Serotonin.** A neurotransmitter that acts as a calming agent

**Sexually transmitted diseases (STD).** A disease or infection that is contracted through sexual contact

**Spark notes.** Free online study guides

**Stress.** Outside worries that affect the individual

**Substance abuse.** Overindulgence in material that is harmful

**Synaptic connection.** Communication between two neurons

**Temporal lobes.** A part of the brain involved in hearing and memory

**Testosterone.** A male hormone required for sperm production and secondary sexual characteristics such as pubic hair and a lower voice

**Text messaging.** Writing and receiving short messages on mobile phones

**URL.** Address of a site on the Internet

**YouTube.** A free video-sharing website

# REFERENCES

ACT for Youth Upstate Center of Excellence. 2002. Adolescent brain development. Cornell University. www.actforyouth.net (accessed June 7, 2006).
———. 2002. Peers. Cornell University. www.actforyouth.net (accessed June 7, 2006).
———. 2002. Research facts and findings. Cornell University. www.actforyouth.net (accessed June 7, 2006).
———. 2002. Risk, protection and resilience. Cornell University. www.actforyouth.net (accessed June 7, 2006).
Adolescent smoking statistics. 2003. Smoking and teens. American Lung Association www.lungusa.org/tobaccoteensindex.html.
After school for America's teens: A national survey of teen attitudes and behaviors in the hours after school. 2001. YMCA of the USA Drug Policy Alliance. www.drugpolicy.org/library/bibliography/afterschool (accessed March 26, 2004).
Aguilera, A., R. Selgas, R. Codoceo, and A. Bajo. 2000. Uremic anorexia: A consequence of persistently high brain serotonin levels? The tryptophan/serotonin disorder hypothesis. *Peritoneal Dialysis International* 20(6): 810–16.
Amen, D. G. 2002. *Healing ADD: The breakthrough program that allows you to see and heal the six types of attention deficit disorder.* New York: G. P. Putnam's Sons.

Anderson, D. R., A. C. Huston, K. L. Schmitt, D. L. Lineberger, and J. C. Wright. 2002. *Early childhood television viewing and adolescent behavior,* edited by W. F. Overton. Monograph of the Society for Research in Child Development. Boston, MA: Blackwell.

Baird, A. A., S. A. Gruber, D. A. Fein, L. C. Mass, R. J. Steingard, P. F. Renshaw, B. M. Cohen, and D. A. Yurgelun-Todd. 1999. Functional magnetic resonance imaging of facial affect recognition in children and adolescents. *Journal of the American Academy of Child and Adolescent Psychiatry* 38(2): 195–99.

Barbarich, N. 2002. Is there a common mechanism of serotonin dysregulation in anorexia nervosa and obsessive compulsive disorder? *Eating and Weight Disorders* 7(3): 221–31.

Bartels, A., and S. Zeki. 2000. The neural basis of romantic love. *Neuroreport* 11(17): 3829–34.

Beck, A. T., A. J. Rush, B. F. Shaw, and G. Emery. 1979. *Cognitive therapy of depression.* New York: Guilford Press.

Benson, P. L., J. Galbraith, and P. Espeland. 1998. *What kids need to succeed: Proven practical ways to raise good kids.* Minneapolis, MN: Free Spirit.

Bloom, F. E., M. F. Beal, and D. J. Kupfer, D. J. 2003. *The Dana guide to brain health.* New York: Free Press.

Bond-Zielinski, C. n.d. Restraint from sexual activity: How can parents help? Ohio State University Fact Sheet. http://ohioline.osu.edu/flm99fs16.html (accessed April 7, 2006).

Bor, J. S., C. Hynes, J. Van Horn, S. Grafton, and W. Sinnott-Armstrong. 2006. Consequences, action, and intention as factors in moral judgments: An fMRI investigation. *Journal of Cognitive Neuroscience* 18(5): 803–17.

Bowman, L., and S. Howard. 2004. New research shows stark differences in teen brains. www.deathpenaltyinfo.org/article.php?scid=27&did=1000 (accessed April 7, 2006).

Bremner, J. D. 2005. *Does stress damage the brain? Understanding trauma-related disorders from a neurological perspective.* New York: W. W. Norton.

Brendtro, L., M. Brokenleg, and S. VanBockern. 2002. *Reclaiming youth at risk.* Bloomington, IN: National Educational Service.

Brown, L. K., K. J. Lourie, G. Zlotnick, and J. Coh. 2000. Impact of sexual abuse on the HIV-risk-related behavior of adolescents in intensive psychiatric treatment. *American Journal of Psychiatry* 157:1413–15.

Brown, S. A., S. F. Tapert, E. Granhom, and D. C. Delis. 2000. Neurocognitive function of adolescents: Effects of protracted alcohol use. *Alcoholism: Clinical and Experimental Research* 24:164–71.

Caldwell, L. C., A. D. Schweinsburg, B. J. Nagel, V. C. Barlett, S. A. Brown, and S. F. Tapert. 2005. Gender and adolescent alcohol use disorders on BOLD (blood oxygen level dependent) response to spatial working memory. *Alcohol and Alcoholism* 40(3): 194–200.

Canadians against Child Abuse Society. Parenting adolescents. www.cacas.ca/reference.htm (accessed April 7, 2006).

Carskadon, M. A. 2002. *Adolescent sleep patterns*. Cambridge: Cambridge University Press.

Chambers, C. D., M. A. Bellgrove, M. G. Stokes, T. R. Henderson, H. Garavan, I. H. Robertson, A. P. Morris, and J. B. Mattingley. 2006. Executive "brake failure" following deactivation of human frontal lobe. *Journal of Cognitive Neuroscience* 18(3): 444–55.

Clark, A. S. 2006. This is your brain online. *CBS NEWS*, June 14.

Clark, L. 2002. Raising responsible youth. http://ohioline.osu.edu/flm02/FS10.html (accessed April 7, 2006).

D'Arcangelo, M. 2000. How does the brain develop? A conversation with Steven Peterson. *Educational Leadership* 58(3): 68–71.

Damasio, A. R. 2003. *Looking for Spinoza: Joy, sorrow, and the feeling brain*. New York: Harcourt.

Davis, J. L. 2003. Teenagers: Why do they rebel? www.webmd.com/content/Article/72/81675.htm (accessed July 7, 2006).

De Bellis, M. D., D. B. Clark, S. R. Beers, P. H. Soloff, A. M. Boring, J. Hall, A. Kersh, and M. S. Keshavan. 2000. Hippocampal volume in adolescent-onset alcohol use disorders. *American Journal of Psychiatry* 157:737–44.

Delfos, M. F. 2004. *Children and behavioural problems: Anxiety, aggression, depression, ADHD—A biopsychological model with guidelines for diagnostics and treatment*. London: Jessica Kingsley.

Duke University Medical Center. 2004. Prenatal nicotine primes adolescent brain for addiction. www.dukehealth.org (accessed July 7, 2006).

Edgette, J. S. 2002. *Negotiating with your teen.* New York: Perigee.

Eichenbaum, H. E., and N. J. Cohen. 2001. *From conditioning to conscious recollection.* Upper Saddle River, NJ: Oxford University Press.

Fairburn, C. G., and P. J. Harrison. 2003. Eating disorders. *Lancet* 361:407–16.

Feinberg, T. E., and J. P. Keenan. 2005. *The lost self.* Oxford: Oxford University Press.

Feingold, A. 1996. Cognitive gender differences: Where are they and why are they there? *Learning and Individual Differences* 8:25–32.

Feinstein, S. G. 2004. *Secrets of the teenage brain.* Thousand Oaks, CA: Corwin Press.

———. 2006. *The Praeger handbook on learning and the brain.* Westport, CT: Praeger.

Fisher, H. E., A. Aron, D. Mashek, H. Li, and L. L. Brown. 2002. Defining the brain systems of lust, romantic attraction, and attachment. *Archives of Sexual Behavior* 31(5): 413–19.

Gardner, A. 2004. Fast food linked to obesity, insulin problems. *HealthDayNews* [online]. www.healthfinder.gov/news/newsstory.asp?docID =523168 (accessed October 25, 2005).

Gazzaniga, M. S., R. B. Ivry, and G. T. Mangum, eds. 2002. *Cognitive neurosciences.* 2nd ed. New York: W. W. Norton.

Gee, J. P. 2003. *What video games have to teach us about learning and literacy.* New York: Palgrave Macmillan.

Giedd J. N., J. Blumenthal, N. O., Jeffries, F. X. Castellanos1, H. Liu, A. Zijdenbos, T. Paus, A. C. Evans, and J. L. Rapoport. 1999. Brain development during childhood and adolescence: A longitudinal MRI study. *Nature Neuroscience* 2:861–63.

Goleman, D. 2002. *Primal leadership: Realizing the power of emotional intelligence.* Boston: Harvard Business School.

Hall, J. 2005. Neuroscience and education What can brain science contribute to teaching and learning? The SCRE Centre, University of Glasgow. www.scre.ac.uk/spotlight (accessed July 1, 2006).

Hamilton, M. A., and S. F. Hamilton. 2005. Mentoring. Research Facts and Findings. ACT. www.actforyouth.net (accessed June 28. 2006).

Holmes, L. 2001. Heavy video game use by kids may slow brain development. *The Observer* (London), August 19.

How can research on the brain inform education? SCIMAST Classroom Compass. Southwest Educational Development Laboratory. www.sedl .org/scimath/compass/v03n02/1.html (accessed April 7, 2006).

Johnston, K., and S. Everling. 2006. Neural activity in monkey prefrontal cortex is modulated by task context and behavioral instruction during delayed-match-to-sample and conditional prosaccade-antisaccade tasks. *Journal of Cognitive Neuroscience* 18(5): 749–65.

Juvenile Justice Center. 2004. *Adolescence, brain development and legal culpability*. Chicago: American Bar Association.

Kanwisher, N., and M. Moscovitch. 2000. The cognitive neuroscience of face processing: An introduction. *Cognitive Neuropsychology* 17(1–3): 1–11.

Klimek, D., and M. Anderson. 1987. Understanding and parenting adolescent. Ann Arbor, MI: ERIC Clearinghouse on Counseling and Personnel Services. ED 291018.

Kim, J., and D. Diamond. 2002. The stressed hippocampus, synaptic plasticity and lost memories. *Nature Reviews Neuroscience* 3(6): 453–62.

LeDoux, J. 1996. *The emotional brain: The mysterious underpinnings of emotional life*. New York: Simon & Schuster.

Lerner, R., A. L. Brennan, E. R. Noh, and C. Wilson. The parenting of adolescents and adolescents as parents: A developmental contextual perspective. http://parenthood.library.wisc.edu/Lerner/Lerner.html (accessed April 7, 2006).

Lewis, M. D., C. Lamm, S. J. Segalowitz, J. Stieben, and P. D. Zelazo. 2006. Neurophysiological correlates of emotion regulation in children and adolescents. *Journal of Cognitive Neuroscience* 18(3): 430–43.

MacDonald, A. 2003. Imaging studies bring ADHD into sharper focus [online]. *Brainwork: The Neuroscience Newsletter* 13(2). www.dana .org/pdf/periodicals/brainwork_0403.pdf (accessed June 25, 2005).

McVeigh, T. 2001. Computer games stunt teen brains. *Observer* (London), August 19.

MedicalPlus Medical Encyclopedia: Adolescent development. www.nim .nih.gov/medlineplus/ency/article/002003.htm (accessed April 7, 2006).

Michigan State University. 2006. Violent video games lead to brain activity characteristic of aggression, MSU researcher shows. www.news-room.msu.edu (accessed July 7, 2006).

Moore, K. A., L. Guzman, E. Hair, L. Lippman, and S. Garrett. 2004. Parent-teen relationships and interactions: Far more positive than not. *Child Trends* 25:1–8.

National Clearinghouse on Families and Youth. Supporting your adolescent: Tips for parents. www.ncfy.com/publications/tips/tips.htm (accessed April 7, 2006).

Parenting adolescents (president's page). 2004. *Indian Pediatrics* 41:887–90.

Pechmann, C., L. Levine, S. Loughlin, and F. Leslie. 2005. Impulsive and self-conscious: Adolescents' vulnerability to advertising and promotion. *American Marketing Association* 24(2): 202–21.

Phelan, T. W. 1998. *Surviving your adolescents.* Glenn, IL: Child Management.

Phillips, P. E. M., G. D. Stuber, M. L. A. V. Heien, R. M. Wightman, and R. M. Carell. 2003. Subsecond dopamine release promotes cocaine seeking. *Nature* 422: 614–18.

Ponton, L. 2000. *The sex lives of teenagers.* New York: Penguin Group.

Public Broadcasting Station. 2002 Frontline: Interviews inside the teenage brain [online]. www.pbs.org/wgbh/pages/frontline/shows/teenbrain (accessed July 6, 2005).

Rabinowicz, T., D. E. Dean, J. M. Petetot, and G. M. de Courten-Myers. 1999. Gender differences in the human cerebral cortex: More neurons in males; more processes in females. *Journal of Child Neurology* 14(2): 98–107.

Restak, R. M. 2003. *The new brain: How the modern age is rewiring your mind.* New York: Rodale Press.

Sach, S. L. 1996. Communicating with your teen. Ohio State University Extension Fact Sheet, Families Meeting the Challenge. http://ohioline.osu.edu/hyg-fast/5000/5157.html (accessed July 1, 2006).

———. 1996. Monitoring: Staying involved in your teen's life. Ohio State University Extension Fact Sheet, Families Meeting the Challenge. http://ohioline.osu.edu/hyg-fast/5000/5157.html (accessed July 1, 2006).

Santrock, J. W. 2007. *Adolescence.* 11th ed. New York: McGraw-Hill.

Sells, S. P. 2001. *Parenting your out-of-control teenager.* New York: St. Martin's Griffin.

Spano, S. 2004. Stages of adolescent development. ACT for Youth Up-state Center of Excellence Research Facts and Findings. www.human .cornell.edu/actforyouth (accessed June 28, 2006).

Steinberg, L. 2001. We know some things: Parent-adolescent relation-ships in retrospect and prospect. *Journal of Research on Adolescence* 11(1): 1–19.

Stilwell, B., M. Galvin, S. M. Kopta, and S. Kopta. 2000. *Right vs. wrong: Raising a child with a conscience.* Bloomington: Indiana University Press.

Strauch, B. 2004. *The primal teen: What the new discoveries about the teenage brain tell us about our kids.* New York: Bantam Dou-bleday.

Sullivan, E. V., R. Fama, M. J. Rosenbloom, and A. Pfefferbaum. 2002. A profile of neuropsychological deficits in alcoholic women. *Neuropsychology* 16:74–83.

Tancredi, L. R. 2005. *Hardwired behavior: What neuroscience reveals about morality.* New York: Cambridge University Press.

Tapert, S. F., and G. G. Brown. 1999. Neuropsychological correlates of adolescent substance abuse: Four-year outcomes. *Journal of the International Neuropsychological Society* 5:481–93.

Tapert, S. F., A. D. Schweinsburg, V. C. Barlett, M. J. Meloy, S. A. Brown, G. G. Brown, and L. R. Frank. 2004. BOLD response and spatial work-ing memory in alcohol use disordered adolescents. *Alcoholism: Clinical and Experimental Research* 28:1577–86.

The teen brain: Thrills, peers, and stress. The teen brain: Implications for pediatric nurses. www.medscape.com/viewarticle/504350_5 (accessed July 7, 2006).

Toye, S. 2001. *Study shows obesity bad for the mind, too. Science Daily* [online]. www.sciencedaily.com/releases/2001/05/010529071515.htm (accessed June 24, 2005).

Uttal, W. R. 2001. *The new phrenology: The limits of localizing cognitive processes in the brain.* Boston: MIT Press.

Walsh, D. 2004. *Why do they act that way? A survival guide to the ado-lescent brain for you and your teen.* New York: Free Press.

Wang, G. J., et al. 2001. Brain dopamine and obesity. *Lancet,* 357(9253): 354–57.

Weinberger, D. R., B. Elvevag, and J. N. Giedd. 2005. The adolescent brain: A work in progress. The National Campaign to Prevent Teen Pregnancy. www.teenpregnancy.org (accessed July 7, 2006).

Welker, E. 1998. Understanding teens: Opening the door to a better relationship. The Ohio State University Extension. http://ohioline.osu.edu/flm98/fs04.html (accessed April 7, 2006).

White, A. M. Alcohol and the adolescent brain. www.duke.edu/~amwhite/Adolescence/adolescent6.html (accessed July 7, 2006).

Wolf, A. E. 2002. *Get out of my life, but first could you drive me and Cheryl to the mall?* New York: Farrar, Straus & Giroux.

Yovel, G., and B. Duchaine. Specialized face perception mechanisms extract both part and spacing information: Evidence from developmental prosopagnosia. *Journal of Cognitive Neuroscience* 18(4): 580–93.

# INDEX

abstract thinking, 7, 86
abuse, 9, 26, 28, 39, 60, 123,
   125–26, 127
acne, 11, 74, 75
ADD/ADHD, 12, 63, 118–21
addiction, 10, 98, 102, 110–16
adrenaline, 70
aggression, 63, 67, 102, 103, 116,
   117, 118, 129
alcohol, 10, 38, 43, 49, 52, 59, 62,
   72, 77, 110, 111, 112–16, 118,
   124
amygdala, 9, 20, 25, 27, 28, 65, 67,
   97, 102, 117, 123
androgens, 73
anger, 22, 65, 67, 72, 116, 117,
   118
anorexia nervosa, 77, 78
anxiety, 88, 128, 129
argue, 11, 62, 63, 64, 89, 118, 126
athletic, 111, 126

autonomy, 11, 32, 56, 68, 94, 148
axons, 4

basal ganglia, 120
body image, 74, 75, 104
body language, 23, 27, 41
break-up, 53, 55
bulimia, 77, 78

CD, 91, 101
cell phone, 48, 92, 101, 107, 108
clique, 50
clothing, 52, 75
communication, 10, 26, 27, 29, 33,
   57, 66, 105, 108, 117
computer, 78, 75, 100, 101,
   103,104, 105, 107, 108, 119,
   120, 129
conformity, 49, 50, 148
corpus callosum, 46, 99, 125
cortex, 27, 61, 91, 97, 107, 124

# ABOUT THE AUTHOR

**Sheryl Feinstein**, Ed.D. is an associate professor at Augustana College in Sioux Falls, South Dakota. She is the author of the book, *Secrets of the Teenage Brain* (2004). She is also the editor and co-author of *The Praeger Handbook of Learning and the Brain* (2006) and *Teaching the At-Risk Teenage Brain* (2007). In the summer of 2006, she was a fellow at Oxford's Harris Manchester College and conducted research in the area of cognitive neuroscience with the adolescent. Sheryl is a Fulbright Scholar lecture/researcher to Tanzania, 2007–2008.

In addition to teaching at Augustana College, she consults at a correctional facility for adolescent boys and at a separate site for Emotionally/Behaviorally Disturbed (EBD) adolescents in Minnesota. The correctional facility has received state and local recognition for their exemplary practices and service.

Prior to being at Augustana College, Sheryl taught in the public schools and was a curriculum consultant for a K–12 school district in Minnesota. She also started an alternative school for high school students and was a regional liaison in Minnesota to facilitate integrating national and state standards into alternative programs. She presents nationally and internationally on the adolescent brain. More importantly, she is the mother of four children.